CZECHOSLOVAKIA

(VISTULA R.)

POLAND

N
W E
S

(ODER R.)

Katowice

WISŁA R.

Kruków

rnov
Opava

Ostrava
Orlová
Český Těšín

ičín
ranice
Frýdek-Místek

Vsetín

Žilina
Ružomberok

Prešov

valdav

Martin
Spišská Nová Ves

Trenčín

Banská Bystrica
Michalovce
Uzhgorod

SLOVAKIA
Košice

Zvolen
Čierná
nad Tisou
Chop

U. S. S. R.

WITRA R.

ava
Rimavská Sobota

Nitra
Banská Štiavnica

Lučenec

Levice

Nové Zámky

Kolárovo
DANUBE R.

Komárno

HUNGARY

RUMANIA

BUDAPEST

A Year Is Eight Months

A YEAR IS EIGHT MONTHS

by
Journalist M

Introduction by Tad Szulc

DOUBLEDAY & COMPANY, INC., GARDEN CITY, NEW YORK

1970

Originally published in German as
DIE KNOTROLLIERTE RIVOLUTION.
Paul Zsolnay Verlag, © *1969 Paul Zsolnay Verlag*

Library of Congress Catalog Card Number 75–87102
Introduction and Translation Copyright © *1970 by*
Doubleday and Company, Inc.
Printed in the United States of America
First Edition in the United States of America

Editor's Note: All notes marked with an asterisk were added by the editor in order to explain points that might otherwise have been obscure to the American reader.

Introduction

Journalist M is an old acquaintance of mine, a man of wisdom and courage, and, inevitably, an optimist when it comes to the future of Czechoslovakia still occupied by the Soviet troops. I must say from the outset that M—a Kafkaesque pseudonym in the best Czech tradition—has been a Communist since his early adulthood, but a Communist so idealistic, even romantic, that over the long years of Moscow's tortuous and ideological zigzags he has openly rebelled against what he saw as the immorality and indecency of the Party line. What, I think, makes his book remarkable is that it was written by a true-believer Communist—and not a repentant Marxist or a Western liberal—who found in the 1968 Prague Spring the meaning of Communism for which he had been searching all his life. And it is symbolic of M's attitude that he writes in *A Year Is Eight Months* that the Prague Spring "has been called the last chance of the world Communist movement."

Journalist M, as this Introduction is written in September 1969, remains in Prague—as far as I know. With the powerful pressures of vengeance now mounting in Czechoslovakia against the intellectuals and the journalists who spearheaded the Communist liberalizing experiment of 1968 and the widespread Party purges, I do not believe it wise to identify M any further. Suffice it to say that during the "Eight Months" preceding the Warsaw Pact armies' invasion in August 1968, Journalist M was a highly active and influential member of the Prague newspaper fraternity. I often sought his counsel in the pre-invasion days, and it just so happened that M and I lunched together a few days before the invasion. When we shook hands to say good-bye after the meal, M was full of dire premonitions.

I have seen M on at least one occasion after the Czechoslovak government, acting under foreign pressure, expelled me from the country in December 1968 on ill-contrived charges of military and political espionage, presumably on behalf of my employers, *The New York Times*. The time and the place of our last encounter need not be mentioned, but M was still working in his profession—which he now no longer does—and, oddly, he was still relatively optimistic about the future developments in Czechoslovakia.

M's book ends with an Afterword written in February 1969, which was six months after the invasion. He remarks that a general strike would explode in Czechoslovakia if someone tried to remove from power President Svoboda or Party leader Alexander Dubček. But this was said before the April plenum of the Party's Central Committee fired Dubček and replaced him as First Secretary with Gustav Husák toward whom Journalist M is comparatively gentle in his discussion of the post-invasion period.

M may have been an optimist, but he also was a realist. He therefore asks in the concluding lines of his book: "Will unheard-of pressure and the threats of violence to which the leaders are exposed succeed in 'changing the people,' in making them fall into lethargy and passivity? . . . That," M says, "is the decisive question for Czechoslovakia in the second year of her great awakening that has shaken the world and brought new hope for socialism and democracy."

Another six-month period has elapsed since M wrote his Afterword, but his question still cannot be fully and satisfactorily answered as events in Czechoslovakia keep succeeding each other at a furious pace. In the sense that this Introduction represents a further postscript to M's own Afterword, it must be reported that pressure by the Soviets and the re-emerging Czechoslovak Communist conservatives have succeeded in smashing almost entirely the resistance of the Prague leadership.

There was no visible reaction to Dubček's dismissal and, in fact, many of his erstwhile supporters breathed a sigh of relief when he was consigned to virtual political oblivion. As Journalist M remarks in his book, the Soviets had wanted the pre-invasion leaders to do their "dirty work" for them when they failed to establish a Quisling regime in Prague. Dubček, for one, no longer has to soil his hands and his conscience with the filth of the purges, and for this many of his admirers are thankful.

Since M wrote his book, the Czechoslovak press, radio and television has ceased to be the freest in Communist Europe. Journalist M has himself seen the closing of the liberal publications and the mass firings of the progressive newspapermen from their jobs. If he, indeed, remains in Prague, he may read these days in *Rudé Právo* and other Party publications the attacks and the slander against those, including himself, who made the Prague Spring into the "new hope" for socialism. What he sees in Prague today is melancholy and tragedy.

But does it all mean that the Czechs and the Slovaks have been inexorably and irreversibly pushed into "lethargy and passivity"? The anti-Soviet disturbances in Prague, Brno and other Czechoslovak cities on the first anniversary of the invasion—deliberately provoked or not—showed clearly that the defiant spirit of 1968 is still alive. The obvious inability of Husák and his associates to unite the Communist Party or to extract from the population anything beyond the most begrudged acceptance of the *status quo* guaranteed by 80,000 Soviet troops in the country seems to indicate that the Czechs and the Slovaks are far from a total passivity.

It has been months since I last conversed with Journalist M. I have no way of knowing whether his courageous optimism is still with him. But, for my part, I do not choose to write off the Czechoslovaks, the Prague Spring and all it stood for in terms of a profound challenge to the old dogmas of Marxism and Communism. The Prague experience was too profound, too traumatic, too heroic to be dismissed with a tearful farewell to that which could have been.

The "Eight Months" of 1968 were, I think, much more than just a year in M's title. It was a watershed in Communist history and not a mere episode that historians of the future will regard as a dramatic footnote. There is, I believe, a certain inexorable logic in the workings of history and this logic is bound to assert itself in the long run in Czechoslovakia. The Prague Spring, then, will not have been in vain.

When I last parted from Journalist M, he said: "I know we shall see each other again in better times and in a better Czechoslovakia." I am inclined to believe that it shall be so.

TAD SZULC

Contents

Introduction by Tad Szulc vii

1. *The Rebellion of the Intellectuals* 1

2. *Economic Doldrums* 9

3. *Conflicts between the Two Nations* 16

4. *The Struggle against Police Rule* 23

5. *Change in the Central Committee* 31

6. *Winter Intermezzo* 40

7. *Revolution through Words* 48

8. *New Men to the Fore* 57

9. *The Action Program* 69

10. *The Whole Society Is Shaken* 75

11. *The April Plenary* 83

12. *Thunder on the Horizon*   92

13. *Convocation of the Extraordinary Congress*   102

14. *The "Two Thousand Words"*   112

15. *Change in Slovakia*   123

16. *The Warsaw Ultimatum*   129

17. *"We Are with You—Be with Us"*   141

18. *Still They Negotiate*   145

19. *Ardor and Premonition*   153

20. *The Night of the Tanks*   157

21. *Political and Moral Bankruptcy: The Occupation*   167

Afterword: February 1969   178

Chronology   187

Bibliography   195

Index   199

A Year Is Eight Months

Chapter 1

The Rebellion of the Intellectuals

In the summer of 1966 a Czech journalist on a visit to Oslo was startled when one of the editors of a leading Norwegian liberal daily asked him: Why is Czechoslovakia the most Stalinist country in Eastern Europe?

The journalist argued that the contrary was true, at least as far as concepts, ideas and ideological controversy were concerned: Czechoslovakia, of all the countries of Eastern Europe, had done most to break the monolithic character of Stalinist dogmatism and conservatism. He was so convincing that the Norwegian decided to write an article on the subject for his newspaper.

To be sure, superficially Czechoslovakia, a little country in the heart of Europe, seemed deeply Stalinist until the end of 1967, despite its cultural traditions and democratic past. Under Antonín Novotný, it was governed by a rigid, centralized bureaucratic system controlled by a small group of Communist Party politicians; its foreign policy slavishly followed Moscow's instructions; its secret police was all-powerful; its economy was stagnant, and the majority of its people were apathetic toward public affairs.

But beneath this surface was a great deal of ferment. Ever since Stalin's death, and particularly since 1956, the dogmatic Party leadership had been alternately retreating and weakening the dictatorial aspects of the regime under pressure, and counterattacking with new repressions and a tightening of its rule. A groundswell of new ideas, which encompassed all Czechoslovak intellectuals, prepared for the changes that took place at the end of 1967, when the Communist Party itself had to give way to the mounting social conflict and abandon its Stalinist leadership. This in turn made it possible for a broadly based mass movement to develop, which sought for a synthesis of socialism and democracy, "socialism with a human face."

Czechoslovakia lies at the crosscroads of East and West. Thus it has always been a place of strong ideological cross-currents, where various ideas and philosophies clash. As soon as the Iron Curtain that had isolated this crossroads from all contact with the West was raised even a little, fresh winds again began to freshen the stale atmosphere of dogmatism.

The first chance came with Khrushchev's reluctant renewal of contacts with Yugoslavia. From the nineteenth century on, the Czechs and Slovaks had had traditionally friendly relations with their Slav neighbors, and the break in 1948 was strongly felt. But at that time Stalin's authority was so great that his verdict was considered final and was voluntarily accepted by Communist intellectuals when the Communist Party came to power in Czechoslovakia. In 1956, under Khrushchev, the "traitor and fascist" Tito was again welcomed into the family of socialist leaders. For the first time, the hierarchy was forced to apologize to a heretic and to recind the edict by which he had been excommunicated and damned. If one anti-heretical edict was recinded, why not others?

In February 1956 came the Twentieth Congress of the Soviet Communist Party and Khrushchev's speech detailing Stalin's crimes. After returning from Moscow, Novotný had to admit publicly that "the cult of personality" and "non-adherence to socialist legality" (as the dictatorship and its terrible crimes were euphemistically called) had also afflicted Czechoslovakia in the early fifties. But because Novotný himself had participated in these crimes, building his political career around them, he publicly announced that, although Rudolf Slánský and the other politicians executed in 1952 after mock trials were not guilty of the crimes for which they were sentenced, they were nevertheless guilty of other, unspecified crimes and would therefore not be rehabilitated.*

The shock caused by the Twentieth Congress shook the entire Czechoslovak Communist Party. For the first time since 1948 stormy Communist Party meetings were held, where intellectuals and workers demanded public discussion of all Party policy and the convocation of an Extraordinary Congress of the Party. They demanded that this Congress evaluate the whole past period and remove those leaders who had been responsible for the crimes and mistakes of the past. The Party leadership and its apparatus had to fight back, to retreat, to maneuver, to try to outsmart its critics. The stormy events of autumn 1956 in Poland and Hungary finally helped the Novotný group suppress the coming rebellion. The Hungarian "counterrevolution" and the Soviet intervention in Budapest, together with Moscow's renewed attack upon Yugoslav "revisionism," fortified the Stalinists' position. The Party membership again became apathetic and the Party apparatus again omnipotent. A campaign was started against "revisionism." (In 1956 "revisionism" had been most apparent in ideological matters and in the writings of some philosophers, mainly Karel Kosík and Ivan Sviták, as well as in the literary weekly of the Writers' Union, the *Literární noviny*.)

Until the 1960s, Novotný's regime was supported by the country's economic situation. Czechoslovakia had the highest living standard in Eastern Europe, the economy was growing, and tourists from the Soviet Union, Poland, and Rumania still looked to Czechoslovakia as the America of the socialist world. As a whole, the population, especially the working class, was not yet disgruntled. The bankruptcy of the official ideology was felt

* Political rehabilitation consisted, first, in publicly clearing the reputations of the accused, in some cases of restoring their Party memberships and, by 1968, of monetary compensation for their years in prison. In August 1963 Slánský's conviction was reversed, but he was only partially rehabilitated. Ed.

mostly by the intelligentsia, especially creative artists and social scientists, among whom the worm of disillusionment, disappointment and discontent continually undermined the positions of Stalinism.

After 1961 Czechoslovakia's economic position began to deteriorate. In the USSR, the Twenty-second Soviet Party Congress revealed further mistakes of the period of the "cult of personality." Novotný's regime was forced to retreat further. Thus, in 1963, a special commission of the Central Committee of the Czechoslovak Party was appointed, composed of historians, lawyers and members of the Party apparatus, to re-examine the case of the "Slovak nationalists" sentenced in 1954 to long prison terms. The commission was known as the Barnabitky Commission, after a former convent in Prague where it met. The Slovak "bourgeois nationalists" were well-known Communists, leaders of the Party during World War II and organizers of the Slovak national uprising against the Nazis in 1944. The most famous of them, the poet Ladislav Novomeský and the former President of the Slovak autonomous government, Gustav Husák, had recently been released from prison, but the stigmata of treason and of "bourgeois nationalism" were still upon them. The Barnabitky Commission, after several months spent examining hundreds of documents, found the accused completely innocent of nationalism and rehabilitated them. The regime was forced to restore their citizen's rights, but they were not allowed to participate in political life.

The work of the Barnabitky Commission gave significant impetus to the development of the social sciences in Czechoslovakia. Historians began to investigate the recent history of the country and of the Communist Party unblinkered by the charismatic distortion of Stalinist dogmatism, and thus helped to remove the web of lies and legends that Stalinism had spun. Philosophers critically re-evaluated the official theories of dialectical materialism and took an interest in the writings of such unorthodox Marxists as Antonio Gramsci, Jean-Paul Sartre, Erich Fromm, Herbert Marcuse and Ernst Fischer. Economists, led by Professor Ota Šik, began to criticize the system of command planning, which followed exactly the Soviet model, and searched for ways to combine a planned economy with the functions of a market economy. Sociology, which during Stalin's lifetime was considered a "bourgeois demi-science" and therefore completely suppressed, became the central interest of young social scientists, who read extensively American and German sociological theories. Lawyers and political scientists took a skeptical view of the monolithic society that had grown up under contemporary socialism and began to rethink the problems of democratic pluralism.

While this revolution in ideas first made itself felt in academic circles, the first breakthrough in expression took place in the arts. Zhdanov's theories of socialist realism, forced down the throats of Czechoslovak artists after 1948, were by now so obviously outdated and senseless that even official Party spokesmen did not dare to defend them publicly. The rehabilitation of Franz Kafka played a great part in the ideological ferment among Czech and Slovak intellectuals. Writers of literary theory and history took a greater interest in the twenties and thirties, when Czech and Slovak literature (such as Karel Čapek's successful play of 1921, *RUR,* which gave the world the word "robot") was part of the development of modern artistic trends and forms. Works of fiction abandoned "constructive" themes and tried to concern themselves with the problems of modern man. Good Western literature was translated on a huge scale, and the starved book market swallowed it in great quantities. The plays of Czech and Slovak dramatists—Karvaš, Pavlíček, Havel, Kohout—were performed not only at home, but in theaters throughout the world. And then came the "new wave" of Czechoslovak cinema, which surprised the whole world and carried off honors at film festivals everywhere.

This renascence of modern Czechoslovak social science and arts was not simple or straightforward. The Party bureaucracy fought a continuous if retreating battle. Censorship tried to suppress modern thinking and modern ideas. The writings of the younger generation of historians who sought to revise official versions of Party history were refused publication and their authors were reprimanded. A novel by the young writer Josef Škvorecký, *The Cowards,* was taken off the market and the author persecuted; he had difficulty earning a living, and critics who had praised the book lost their own jobs. The activities of the Institute of Philosophy of the Czechoslovak Academy of Sciences, where a number of "revisionists" had been uncovered, were investigated by a special commission set up by the Presidium, and a complete closedown of the Institute was seriously discussed. The ideological secretary of the Party's Central Committee, Václav Slavík, was suspended for being too "liberal": Čestmír Císař took his place, and shortly afterward was displaced for the same reasons by Vladimír Koucký, who in turn was supplanted by Jiří Hendrych—all this during a period of only five years.

The censors forbade the production of domestic and foreign plays, or allowed them to be staged only after suspect lines had been deleted. Courageous articles in which any new idea was taken up were mercilessly censored. The weeklies of the Writers' Union, Prague's *Literární noviny* and Bratislava's *Kulturný život,* always kept on hand a stock of alternative articles to replace censored ones. The Central Committee's ideological secretary reviewed exhibitions before they were opened to the public and personally removed examples of abstract art and paintings officially thought too "modernist."

But censorship and repression could not prevail in the face of a united front of the entire artistic and scientific intelligentsia— especially since the censors were not unduly intelligent or overly educated. Thus, an article written in a somewhat complex style would pass the censors unnoticed. An article in a scientific journal containing many words of foreign origin that the censor did not understand could be printed. A film considered ideologically unsound for domestic viewers and sold abroad for hard currency could be shown at home after a success in the West. The Institute of Philosophy, shortly after being attacked as revisionist, received a state prize for the work of an interdisciplinary team of its social scientists headed by Radovan Richta. The team had studied the social implications of the current world revolution in science and technology, and was now acceptable because its work had been favorably received by the Party leadership for the manner in which it described the development of modern technology and its future usefulness in a Communist society. In 1966, a new weekly magazine of the Journalists' Union, *Reportér,* was allowed to publish a round table discussion of conservatism and dogmatism in the Communist movement. Such men as Eduard Goldstuecker and Jiří Hanzelka participated, and in many ways the round table anticipated the currents that reached full flood in the spring of 1968.

The group around Novotný was helpless against this explosion of ideas. Bureaucrats and careerists, cynics and undereducated men, they could do nothing but retreat step by step, maneuver, try to apply police power again and use demagogy to sow distrust between workers and intellectuals. But it was impossible to stop the torrent of new ideas.

When they tried to do this by harsh measures taken against the Writers' Union in the autumn of 1967, it was already too late. By then the ideological bankruptcy of Stalinism was complete and the contradictions within Czechoslovak society had become very strong—besides the tension between intellectuals and Party, very deep nationalistic and economic problems had developed. Under these pressures an opposition within the Central Committee of the Communist Party crystallized. Becoming aware of the fact that it was heading for disaster, the country rose up against Novotný.

An important reason for this split within the Party was the unbearable atmosphere generated by the First Secretary of the Party and the President of the Republic, Antonín Novotný. A politician of district stature, Novotný had reached the height of power through a web of cross relationships and personal intrigues among members of the highest Party and state bodies. He was neither highly intelligent nor especially capable. He was such a poor speaker that he always read his public speeches, which were written by a number of ghost writers. When he tried to improvise something of his own, he would begin to falter and commit unheard-of atrocities against the rules of Czech grammar. After the death of President Antonín Zápotocký in 1957, Novotný took in his own hands the top powers in both the state and the Party. He was able to maintain these powers by manipulating various personal conflicts and rivalries among the other members of the Presidium. He was always the embodiment of mediocrity, half-educated and without imagination, but through unlimited devotion and obedience he gained support from Big Brother in Moscow.

With the years, Novotný acquired a certain routine in dealing with representatives of other Communist parties or, on rare occasions, Western statesmen: he would impress these dignitaries favorably by his knowledge of some details concerning their own countries—such details having been carefully prepared for him in advance by his staff. With age and experience his arrogance, intolerance and self-assurance grew. He began to make personal, arbitrary decisions about which scientific or literary works to proscribe or allow to be published, in spite of the fact that his own intellectual interests were limited to playing cards with a few close friends. He personally hired and dismissed Cabinet members, ambassadors, Party secretaries. He became accustomed to raising his voice, shouting down members of the Central Committee as well as his colleagues on the Presidium. The enormous personal power concentrated in his hands was applied in a manner that made enemies of his bosom friends. The atmosphere among those in the top posts of government and Party grew heavier until, to his great surprise, Novotný learned that his closest collaborators had conspired against him, and he lived to see a palace revolution sweep him from power.

Chapter **2**

Economic Doldrums

Bohemia and Moravia were the industrial workshops of the Austro-Hungarian Empire, accounting for 70 per cent of all imperial industrial production. During the twenty interwar years of Masaryk's Czechoslovakia, the economy continued to develop even though the country was hard hit by the Depression of 1929–34. During World War II, the Nazis constructed a number of new factories, considering Czechoslovakia safer than the German heartland against Allied air attack. Thus at the war's end, the Czechoslovk economy, especially when compared with the economies of other Central and East European nations, was relatively sound in spite of considerable losses. The postwar period promised great potential for further economic growth.

The country is poor in raw materials and rich in skilled labor. There is a familiar saying that Czech workers and technicians have hands of gold. Czechoslovak industry was strongest where the minimum of raw materials (especially metals) and the maximum of human resources were required. Czechoslovak industry was diversified: iron and steel were produced, there were many machine factories and a developed glass and ceramics industry based on domestic raw materials. Czechoslovakia produced its own textiles, shoes and consumer goods. Exports of these products, mostly to the West, paid for imports of raw materials and food.

The early postwar years of nationalized industry offered a

chance for rapid and extensive growth. A country whose economy had been little disrupted by the war, with a large supply of skilled labor, in the privileged position of a victor with very good contacts in both East and West, possessed all the prerequisites of a future economic boom. Czechoslovakia was the only country in Europe with uranium ore. Its traditional glass, ceramics and other consumer goods industries were intact at a time when such goods were in great demand everywhere. Before the war, Czechoslovak Škoda and Tatra automobiles competed strongly with German, French and Italian cars. After the war, the Fiat and Volkswagen works lay in ruins, and the French Renault was in great difficulties. The Czechoslovak automobile industry could have become the giant of Europe in this field; with the American aid then available, it could have dominated European markets.

This great potential was not realized; it fell victim to the Cold War. After 1948, Czechoslovakia turned toward the East. The Cold War, the Western embargo on trade with Czechoslovakia, the Korean War, the tension in Berlin, the danger of a third World War—all combined to stop foreign trade with the West almost entirely. This was a fatal blow to the Czechoslovak industries that traditionally produced consumer goods for export.

Instead a vision was born, the vision of a small European industrial country that would become the workshop of the huge Eurasian continent stretching from the Elbe River to the South China Sea. Quickly developing its iron and steel mills, its armory and machine factories to supply weapons and equipment for various investment projects, Czechoslovakia was to industrialize Eastern Europe, the Soviet Union and China. This required the fast reconversion of light and consumer goods industries to heavy production, which, supplied with Soviet ores, would turn out machines for the Eastern markets. Thus was born the "iron and steel concept" of the Czechoslovak economy, the basis of the first and second Five-Year Plans.

The iron and steel concept as a necessary attribute of the construction of socialism came into being in the Soviet Union in the period between the wars. The Soviets faced the necessity of quickly industrializing an underdeveloped country, giving priority to heavy industries, to iron and steel mills. The political isolation of the country as well as preparations for war underscored this need. The Soviet concept of giving priority to heavy industry, which degenerated in practice into production for the sake of production, became the basic tenet of the Stalinist model of constructing socialism. Czechoslovakia, which after 1948 entered the Soviet bloc, completely accepted this concept, together with other Soviet "models."

Before 1948, Czechoslovak Communists spoke about a specifically Czechoslovak path to socialism. After Moscow's conflict with Yugoslavia all discussion of specific national paths was labeled revisionist, and "Titoism" became a crime against the state. Anyone who advocated a different development plan for the Czechoslovak national economy based on the growth of the existing consumer goods industry, the development of automobile production and precision machine building by increasing the volume of skilled labor and specialized machinery was charged with treason, tried and sentenced to death or long-term imprisonment. The iron and steel concept was imposed with all the implements at the disposal of the dictatorship.

Until about 1960 the concept seemed sound. Centralized planning, following every detail of the Soviet model, made possible extensive economic growth, the construction of many machine plants, and full employment. Before long, a shortage of labor developed—a shortage filled by more women than had ever been employed in Czechoslovakia. The standard of living was rather low (but in comparison to other socialist countries, relatively high). All projections were being fulfilled and, often, overfulfilled.

Toward the end of the fifties the weaknesses of the Five-Year Plans began to be apparent. Feverish nationalism after 1948 and overemphasis on industrialization almost entirely liquidated crafts and private services and seriously crippled trade. The construction of new homes, municipal transport and railroads was seriously neglected. Shortages of consumer goods weakened workers' incentives. Wages were to a large extent equalized, and official propaganda continually emphasized that only manual labor is important for society; all artistic or scientific intellectual work is parasitic because intellectuals consume what workers produce. Both wage policy and propaganda thus damped incentive to acquire higher skills and better education. Rigid, centralized planning and bureaucratization resulted in production for the sake of production with small attention paid to sales opportunities or consumer demands. By breaking away from Western economies just as these economies entered a phase of integration, technological innovation and automation, Czechoslovak industry became sadly obsolete, out of step with technological progress and essentially halted at its prewar position. Huge military expenditures caused by fears of a new war slowed economic development even more and consequently foreclosed the possibility of raising standards of living.

Then the whole vision of Czechoslovakia as industrial tutor to the East collapsed. In 1961 China, that tremendous, seemingly bottomless market that would forever import Czechoslovak machinery, canceled all orders and even refused to accept delivery of completed equipment ready for shipment. The machines had to be sold to the Soviet Union at a great loss. Attempts to compensate for the loss of China by granting investment credits to Indonesia, Ghana, Guinea, Iraq, etc. soon led to further financial losses. Billions of crowns' worth of credits had, in fact, to be written off.

Economic difficulties came to a head in 1963, when Czechoslovakia was the only socialist country to experience a marked drop in national income. The third Five-Year Plan, construed on the old iron and steel concept and on further extensive development of industry, was never carried out. Technological obsolescence made it extremely difficult, sometimes impossible, for Czechoslovak products to compete in world markets. Stocks of unsalable goods began to grow, yet bureaucratic planning forced enterprises to continue to produce such goods. The drop in living standards began to be felt.

The deteriorating economic situation forced the Party and the government to look for a way out. Because none could be found, they began to pay more attention to the suggestions of a number of economists, especially those working at the Economic Institute of the Academy of Science, headed by Ota Šik.

The basic tenet of Šik's proposal for economic reform was the marriage of socialist planning to a market economy. The Soviet model of socialist planning, conceived for a specific type of underdeveloped country that intended to industrialize very rapidly, was based on a rigid centralized system of command with set limitations on personal and local initiative and an emphasis on extensive (as opposed to intensive) growth. Such a model can succeed only in a country of comparable structure. But where a certain degree of industrialization has already been achieved, where manpower resources have been exhausted, the source of future growth lies in technological innovation, and intensive rather than extensive development. In such circumstances centralization becomes an obstacle. What is needed is decentralized decision making, personal and local initiative, and incentives for socialist entrepreneurship. All this, however, presupposes a market economy. Only, Šik believed, by reviving the market idea and decentralizing decision making could Czechoslovak industry be made interested in innovation and overcoming obsolescence and thus once again become competitive in the world market, thereby resolving the economic crisis. A return to personal initiative and responsibility, plus larger wage differentials, could create a climate in which enterprises would produce not only for the sake of production, to fulfill the requirements of a plan, but also to satisfy consumer demands.

As it customarily greeted all new ideas, the Party leadership received Šik's proposals with great distrust at first. But the economic situation deteriorated to such an extent that a serious drop in living standards threatened to create deep dissatisfaction among the working class—and this the leadership feared most of all. After a certain hesitation, first the Central Committee and later the Thirteenth Congress of the Party in 1966 officially accepted the main principles of Šik's economic reform.

But here again the basic conservatism of the Novotný leadership, and its inefficiency, became apparent. The kernel of the Šik reform was to do away with bureaucratic chains of command, to encourage personal initiative and to decentralize management. But how could a regime based on the concentration of power in the hands of a few individuals undertake such a reform? How was it possible to withdraw from the omnipotent Presidium and its subordinate Ministries the right to decide the smallest details of economic management, when they had become accustomed to such power? Previously, the Presidium and the Ministries had decided everything—including such questions as which journalist from which newspaper would be permitted to cover an event abroad, or whether Prague hairdressers should or should not obtain a 5 per cent wage increase. The centralization of decision making had in fact reached such a nonsensical level that these matters appeared on the agenda of the Presidium and the Party Secretariat, whose members consequently had no time or energy left to resolve more important, complicated problems.

Thus the principles of the Šik reform were accepted, but immediately stripped of a number of important effects by halfway measures. In principle, decentralization was accepted; in fact, the old system was confirmed. The whole machinery of centralized planning was kept intact—the more so as the vested personal interests of thousands of Party and government bureaucrats, who were threatened by the loss of well-paid jobs, came into play. Thus the reform, designed to cure the economy quickly, ran into a blind alley. Halfway measures and unsystematic remedies could only worsen the situation.

This temporizing was aggravated by Antonín Novotný's deep and reasonable fear that the breakdown of bureaucratic power in the economy would lead to the breakup of bureaucratic power in society as a whole, and begin a democratic development that would eventually undermine both the regime and his personal power. Therefore Novotný did not want to permit the author of the draft of the reform, Professor Ota Šik, to speak at the Thirteenth Congress of the Party, although the Congress was to vote on the draft. Eventually he had to give in and let Šik speak. When Šik, after receiving a standing ovation from the delegates, clearly stated that the success of the reform depended on a parallel political reform—in other words, on a democratization of the whole society and above all of the Party itself—the President of the Republic and First Secretary of the Party became the head censor. Novotný personally cut all important statements from Šik's Congress speech before publication.

Partial economic reform did not solve the economic crisis. Existing conflicts grew stronger, economic difficulties multiplied.

Chapter **3**

Conflicts between the Two Nations

History followed different courses in the two fraternal nations of the Czechs and the Slovaks. During the Middle Ages, the Czechs had their own state and lived through the first great revolution of the new age in the fifteenth and sixteenth centuries, influenced by the teachings of Jan Hus. In the Thirty Years' War they lost their independence, were subjugated for three centuries to the Habsburg monarchy and became the object of great Germanic cultural and economic pressure.* In the nineteenth century the nation went through a cultural renascence. Thus, the Czechs came to the threshold of the twentieth century as a fully developed nation with diversified social classes, a mature culture, a largely urbanized population, and great democratic traditions.

After the tenth century, under the influence of the Magyars, the Slovaks lived in quite different economic and cultural surroundings than did the Czechs. The beginning of the twentieth century found them only just awakening to their national identity. They were a country of peasants suppressed by Hungarian feudal lords, without an urban bourgeoisie, and a thin stratum of intelligentsia, mostly Catholic priests. A small group of patriots,

* The Czechs were intensely aware of the position they occupied in the heart of Europe; Bismarck's comment that "He who controls Bohemia controls Europe" captured the appeal of Czechoslovakia to empire builders. Ed.

schoolteachers and writers dreamed of brotherhood with the Czech nation, while a tiny Protestant minority even used Czech as their church language.

The state of Czechoslovakia was born in 1918 as the country of the united Czech and Slovak nations. Tomáš Masaryk and Eduard Beneš persuaded the Western statesmen who carved up the old map of Europe that in the new republic this united nation would enjoy a wide majority over the German and Hungarian minorities. The illusion of a united nation grew from the idealistic Pan-Slavism preached by the German philosopher Herder, from the close affinity of both languages, Czech and Slovakian, and from political considerations. During the twenty interwar years of Masaryk's republic, Slovakia with the help of the Czechs underwent great cultural and economic development. The cities and towns had a Slovak majority, Slovak culture flourished. Different classes were precipitated out of the newly active society, and the role of Slovak intellectuals grew enormously.

Along with this, a specific Slovak national consciousness also developed. The illusion of a united Czechoslovak nation was rejected, and Slovaks demanded the recognition of a separate, self-contained Slovak state. The advent of the German Nazi movement strengthened centrifugal nationalistic tendencies, which were most manifest in the Slovak Catholic People's Party. The Munich agreement that carved up Czechoslovakia resulted in Slovakian autonomy; after Hitler's occupation of Bohemia and Moravia, Slovakia became a quasi-independent state in which the clero-fascist government was Hitler's puppet.

In 1944, as the coming defeat of Nazi Germany became evident and the battle lines drew nearer to Slovakia, the Communist Party—together with other anti-fascist and democratic groups—organized a Slovak national uprising, its goal the reestablishment of the Czechoslovak republic. National consciousness had by this time grown to such an extent that the program of the Slovak National Council, which led the uprising [and of which Gustav Husák was the most important leader–Ed.], spoke of Slovak self-determination and demanded that the future free

Czechoslovakia be a federation of two republics, Czech and Slovak.

The Slovaks abandoned their demand for federalization in the face of the resistance of President Beneš, who still adhered to the theory of one Czechoslovak nation. But they gained a large measure of autonomy after the Liberation: a separate parliament, the Slovak National Council, and a separate autonomous government located in Bratislava.

In 1948 the Communists came to power* and, soon afterward, the break with Yugoslavia occurred. "Bourgeois nationalism" became a specter invoked by Stalin to tighten his hold on the East European peoples in order to prevent a further disintegration of the Soviet bloc. All theories of independent and specific national paths toward socialism were abandoned. The Soviet system of centralized command became the compulsory model for all socialist countries. One of its first victims was the concept of Slovak autonomy.

In theory, the principle of a self-contained Slovak nation was not questioned. But a regime in which centralist and bureaucratic methods were growing ever stronger could not afford any division of power between Prague and Bratislava. One by one, the autonomous rights of the Slovaks were revoked.

---

* It may be important to remember that this book is written by a member of the Czechoslovak Communist Party. As commentators have noted (see Eliáš and Netík in *Communism in Europe*, ed. Griffith, vol. 2, Cambridge, Mass.: M.I.T. Press, 1953), Czechoslovak (and Soviet) Communist thinkers regard the bloodless "February Revolution" of 1948 as a unique Czechoslovak contribution to the theory and practice of communism. It first demonstrated the possibility of a relatively peaceful transition from capitalism to communism. The Czechoslovak Communist Party, too, had been a genuine mass party with a life of its own in the interwar years. In the May 1946 elections the Communists received 38 per cent of the total vote. Breaking down these over-all results, they received 40 per cent in the Czech lands and 30 per cent in Slovakia. Thus over a year before February 1948 the Communists had become the strongest single party, entitled to designate the Premier (Klement Gottwald). The crisis of February that brought them full power depended on the key posts in the government apparatus held by Communists, on the indecision and disunity of other parties, and on the large number of Prague factory workers, armed and politically organized in the Workers' Militia. Ed.

A role in this development was played by personal animosity and rivalry between some Slovak Stalinists on the one hand (their most important representatives were the Premier of the Prague Cabinet Viliam Široký and the Police Minister Karel Bacílek, one of the organizers of the fifties' political trials), and on the other hand, the leaders of the Slovak national uprising who now headed the Slovak autonomous Cabinet. A number of these, notably the chairman of the autonomous Cabinet, Dr. Gustav Husák, and the poet Ladislav Novomeský, were expelled from the Party, jailed and sentenced to long-term imprisonment for "bourgeois nationalism." Slovakia was now governed by conciliatory representatives of the Prague regime.

The new constitution of 1960 did away with almost all autonomous rights of the Slovak parliament and, in fact, abolished the Bratislava Cabinet. Originally, as conceived in 1945, the Slovak National Council had jurisdiction over all domestic matters concerning Slovakia and could veto national laws if they interfered with Slovakian problems. The constitution of 1960 left the Slovak National Council in effect only one right: to supervise wild life reservations in Slovakia, although it also had strictly limited autonomy in educational matters. The Slovak Cabinet became no more than a local representative of the Prague Ministries. Bratislava lost its status as the capital of Slovakia and, as the seat of the western Slovak regional authority, was reduced to one of ten regional centers in the republic. Regional authorities in central Slovakia (in Banská Bystrica) and in eastern Slovakia (in Košice) were directly subordinate to Prague.

The autonomous rights of the Communist Party of Slovakia were similarly severely curtailed. Things went so far that the Slovak Party was deprived of its mouthpiece, its own daily paper; instead Bratislava published a Slovak version of the Prague *Rudé právo,* edited in Prague and translated into Slovak in Bratislava. Although Slovakian universities and institutes of higher learning were turning out many graduates, the centralist regime in Prague gave precedence to Czechs in government service and the diplomatic corps. The Czech regions, industrially more developed, maintained a higher living standard, which caused some labor migration from Slovakia to Bohemia and Moravia. For instance, a sizable proportion of the workers in the Ostrava coal mines and steel mills, as well as construction workers, came from Slovakia. But there were no Slovak schools for their children, and what assimilation took place further hurt Slovak national feelings.

Many new factories were built in Slovakia and new urban centers developed. Many Slovak peasants turned to industrial labor. Official Communist propaganda considered this the ideal method of solving the problem of nationalities. Any foreign delegation visiting Czechoslovakia was taken on an obligatory tour of new Slovak industrial projects, so that it could observe how successfully Socialism solved the problems of nationalities and underdeveloped regions, while Capitalism mercilessly exploited and neglected such areas as southern Italy.

This line of thought did not, however, take into consideration that, the greater the economic development, the higher the level of civilization attained—and the stronger the national consciousness and resentment against suppression of national rights, especially when any defense of such rights is immediately branded "bourgeois nationalism," and when representatives of the nation's most heroic epoch, the uprising against the Nazis, are prosecuted as traitors.

Thus Slovak nationalism grew—even inside the Communist Party. Slovak Communists, under pressure from their own people, more and more often found themselves in conflict with the centralist regime in Prague.

Once again the leading representative of the Prague regime, Antonín Novotný, exacerbated the situation: his coarseness and lack of education were another abrasive to Slovak feelings. When, eventually, he was forced to release Husák, Novomeský and the other leaders of the Slovak national uprising from prison, he still refused to rehabilitate them legally. Not even in 1963, when their rehabilitation was finally promised, would Novotný allow it. Above all, he absolutely refused any broadening of Slovak national rights.

In the summer of 1967, Novotný made an official state visit to Slovakia that did much to increase tension between the nations and became the spark that ignited the fuse under his throne.

He first visited a large textile factory in Rybarpole where he was welcomed in the name of the workers by an elderly woman, long a member of the Party. In accordance with a certain respect plain people pay to those who hold high offices, she addressed him as "Mister President." The guest rudely interrupted her to tell her that he was not "Mister" but "Comrade President," and that people in Slovakia seemed to forget that they were living under socialism, where everyone is "comrade," not "mister." The elderly woman was at a loss for words; an embarrassing silence followed, the workers stunned by Novotný's behavior.

Next Novotný visited the town of Martin, the cradle of the Slovak national movement and the home of the Matica Slovenská, an institution founded more than a century ago, during Hungarian rule, and dedicated to the advancement of Slovak culture, literature and folklore. A visit to the Matica headquarters is part of the ritual of every official visit to Slovakia, in spite of the fact that the Matica's activities were severely curtailed under Novotný. They were even more severely curtailed in 1968. The Matica may now only maintain a museum and a library.

The directors of the Matica, knowing its history, decided to use the occasion of a visit by the President to present their grievances direct to the highest authority: Slovak immigrants in America, out of patriotism and sentiment, had been sending financial help to the Matica along with books and newspapers published by them in the United States. Neither the money nor the books and magazines had ever reached Martin. After listening to these complaints, Novotný lost his temper and began to shout that the money from America was sent by the CIA and earmarked for anti-Communist activities. (The reason the money never arrived in Martin was, of course, that it was held in

Prague because of Czechoslovakia's need for hard currency.)
He went on to say that all printed matter from the United States
was imperialist ideological infiltration.

Then he turned his back, took his wife's hand and departed.
His agitated hosts, wanting to pacify their enraged guest, decided
to send him gifts—old Slovak prints. After a few days the parcel
was returned with the remark, "The addressee has refused re-
ceipt." Thus Antonín Novotný succeeded in insulting the whole
Slovak nation, and even his firmest supporters in Slovakia could
not forgive him that.

Chapter **4**

The Struggle against Police Rule

The renascence of the Czech nation in the nineteenth century was primarily the work of writers, philologists and historians. After the Thirty Years' War had devastated Bohemia and Moravia, crisscrossing the land several times during the first half of the seventeenth century, almost all educated Czechs went into exile. Bohemia was rapidly Germanized, and by the middle of the eighteenth century Czech was only the language of the serfs. The Enlightenment, the influence of the French Revolution and industrial development revived the Czech language, culture and literature; in the nineteenth century, Czech national consciousness was renewed and became the driving force of Czech nationalism. Writers were, therefore, always considered to be the vanguard for the nation's rights—they were its representatives, its living consciousness. Whenever opportunistic politicians tried to collaborate with the Habsburg monarchy, it was always the writers who raised their voices to protest and to urge national liberation. During World War I, when Czech writers issued a manifesto demanding an independent Czechoslovak state, they were the first to cry out against Austria-Hungary. So the tradition grew that the writers were the spiritual leaders of the nation, the voice of its longings.

Czech history has also marked Czech writers in another way. After the Thirty Years' War and the loss of independence, the

Czech nation also lost a majority of its noble families. A nation of peasants, suppressed by new feudal lords of foreign origin and language, saw its national aspirations as the struggle against feudalism and against an alien and Roman Catholic monarchy. This made it open to the influence of radical and democratic ideas, which strongly influenced the flowering of Czech literature in the nineteenth century; even today conservative ideas and thoughts are still the exception in Czech literature. The great majority of writers and poets have always been more closely identified with democratic and, later, socialist political movements.

Between World Wars I and II, while an independent, democratic Czechoslovakia existed, the majority of Czech and Slovak writers joined left-wing movements, and a number of them were members of the Communist Party. The Nazi occupation strengthened this tendency. Czech and Slovak writers therefore enthusiastically welcomed the Soviet army, the victor over fascism. Most of them have been sincere friends of the Soviet Union, and they supported the Communists wholeheartedly when the latter came to power in 1948.

The widespread disillusionment after Stalin's death in 1953 and the Twentieth Congress of the Soviet Party seriously affected Czech writers. They did not abandon their socialist convictions, or give up their friendship for the Soviets, but they were the first to feel the strait jacket of Stalinist dogmatism. Their tradition of close contact with Western cultural trends suffered, and they took the lead in opposing bureaucratic arbitrariness and the nonsensical interference of the censors.

The Second Congress of the Czechoslovak Writers' Union in 1956 became the first public arena for an open conflict between the writers and the Party. This was repeated at the Third Congress in 1962. The Party leadership threatened reprisals, censorship and intimidation; tried to corrupt and to persuade; and had to maneuver and to retreat. The weeklies published by the Writers' Union in Prague and Bratislava [*Literární noviny* and *Kulturný život*] became the platforms for new ideas, for the sharpest criticisms of bureaucracy and dogmatism. They also formed a nucleus of intellectual opposition to the regime. The wearisome, nerve-racking fight against censorship and bureaucratic interference in cultural matters went on for many years.

In June 1967 the Fourth Congress of the Writers' Union was held. By chance, it convened a few days after the Arab-Israeli War erupted. The war influenced the deliberations of the Congress and provided an occasion to bring the conflict between the writers and the Party leadership to a head.

The Novotný government took a completely pro-Arab stand on the war, which they denounced as Israeli aggression, and broke off diplomatic relations with Israel. Anti-Semitic sentiments from the early fifties and from the Slánský trial reappeared in speeches and the press. Though anti-Semitism was abhorrent to the great majority of the Czechoslovaks and ran contrary to the whole spirit of modern Czech history, the Party press did not hesitate to publish articles full of anti-Zionist, in fact anti-Semitic, invective. This infuriated the intellectuals, who had strong sympathies with Israel, a small country threatened with extermination by its large neighbors. Many recalled with a feeling of guilt the terrible fate of Czech Jews during the Nazi occupation. Some drew analogies between the small state of Israel and the small state of Czechoslovakia, both, at different times in history, fighting for their very survival.

In the days just before the Writers' Congress, the editors of *Literární noviny* planned to publish a round-table discussion on the Middle East war, in which four well-known writers who had previously visited Israel and Egypt were to participate. Because the discussion resulted in a pro-Israeli stand by the writers, who were extremely critical of the official policy of the Czechoslovak government, its publication was banned by the censor. The editors and participating writers were extremely annoyed. The night before the Congress, the Communist writers' group met—as it generally did—with representatives of the Party's Central Committee who were to take part in the deliberations of the Congress; this time the meeting centered not on questions of literature and the Congress, but on the

Middle East conflict and the censorship problem. A very sharp
controversy developed between Jiří Hendrych, the Party's ideological secretary and second man in the Party leadership, and
the Communist writers present.

This was the atmosphere in which, next day, the Writers'
Congress began its work. The opening speech of the young
novelist Milan Kundera alluded to the extraordinary role played
by culture and literature in the history of Czechoslovakia, adding
that only the contribution of both the Czech and Slovak nations
to the treasury of world culture justified the separate existences
of two such small central European peoples. Kundera concluded
by saying that the brutal interference of the Party leadership
made it extremely difficult for modern Czech and Slovak culture
to thrive, impossible for them to contribute to world culture,
and thus directly attacked the quintessence of national existence.
The members then voted almost unanimously (two dissenting
votes) to hear the letter of the Soviet writer Andrei Solzhenitzyn,
sent a few weeks earlier to the Soviet Writers' Union, protesting
censorship and the prosecution of progressive writers in the
Soviet Union. Kundera's speech and Solzhenitzyn's letter were
considered outrageous by the Party bureaucrats present; they
left the meeting hall in protest.

The walkout inspired further discussions. One after another,
writers spoke up against censorship, against suppression of individual liberties, against bureaucracy and the arbitrary actions
of the police. Most important were the speeches of three writers,
all members of the editorial board of the *Literární noviny*.

Ivan Klíma compared the recently adopted press law, which
legalized censorship, with the press law issued exactly one hundred years earlier by the Austrian Emperor. He convincingly
demonstrated that under the rule of Franz Joseph the press
enjoyed a much greater degree of freedom than it had under
socialism. A. J. Liehm, the Czech literary critic and historian,
pointed out how nonsensical were the cultural policies of the
Novotný regime, which ranged from the one extreme of extensive censors' decrees and dogmatic *dicta* to the other of

supporting so-called mass culture that was in reality commercialized culture. He argued that a socialist culture must be above all a free culture, true to the principles of socialism.

Then Ludvík Vaculík was given the floor. A young novelist of working class origin from a Communist family and himself a member of the Party, Vaculík is a writer of strong moral conviction who passionately hates hypocrisy and lying. His emotional speech accused the regime of not being able, in twenty years of existence, to solve a single one of the problems that confront man in modern society. He spoke of the hypocrisy, lies and clichés that poisoned the social atmosphere, of the mediocrity people of low intelligence in the Party leadership had established in which only careerists and men of poor character could thrive. He accused the men around Novotný of deliberately stifling talent, of actually infecting the common people with political apathy under the cover of socialist clichés, of spreading petty bourgeois fears of social commitment.

A political scientist could have shown the inconsistency of every sentence in Vaculík's speech. But its strength was not in political analysis, but in its deep emotional and moral rejection of the regime. After Vaculík's speech it suddenly became clear to everyone that the emperor was naked indeed, as the little boy cried out in the Andersen fairy tale.

The Party leadership reacted to the Writers' Congress with a furious counterattack. Novotný toured the country, making speeches about ideological infiltration by capitalists. Censorship forbade publication of the Congress minutes, but the speeches— especially Vaculík's—were circulated in typewritten copies and sold for a price equal to two days' average wages. The Writers' Union publishing house had a good deal of its ration of newsprint taken away. Several writers who had remained faithful to Novotný were rewarded by higher positions. The new Committee of the Writers' Union, to which several progressive writers had not been elected because of pressure from threatening Party bureaucrats, was not certified by Party bodies and thus could not begin to function.

In September 1967 the Central Committee of the Party met. After listening to speeches by Novotný and Hendrych, who did not hesitate to state boldly that the proceedings of the Writers' Congress had been prearranged in Paris and Bonn, the members decided to act against the writers. Ivan Klíma, A. J. Liehm and Ludvík Vaculík were expelled from the Party; Pavel Kohout and Milan Kundera were reprimanded. The worst blow was the completely illegal takeover of the *Literární noviny,* the weekly of the Writers' Union, by the Ministry of Information. Part of the editorial staff was immediately fired, and the rest resigned in protest. The new editor in chief was a mediocre journalist who had nothing in common with literature or culture in general, but was faithful to Novotný and without principles. He filled the new editorial staff with people like himself.

Though he immediately introduced methods that Randolph Hearst might have envied, he was unsuccessful. He paid salaries twice as high as those paid previously, offered authors royalties three times higher than they could get elsewhere, and did not bridle at blackmail in order to obtain articles from prominent people. He even tried to act the progressive and flirted with a bit of opposition, all to no avail.

A miracle took place that surprised even the optimists. There was a readers' boycott, and a unanimous boycott by creative artists, writers, journalists and social scientists. Circulation of *Literární noviny* dropped by three-fourths. Not a single prominent writer or journalist, not even people known to support Novotný or those who out of fear or opportunism disapproved of the Congress speeches, was willing to write for the stolen magazine.

Thus the intellectuals made their resentment of the Novotný regime apparent, and this resentment grew and spread widely among the people when, next, the police treated the students brutally.

The government had done a great deal for higher education, opening new schools that multiplied the number of university students. But at the same time, by introducing wage equalization and systematically glorifying manual labor and vilifying intellectual work, it undermined the social prestige and importance attached to higher education in the minds of ordinary working people. The conservatism and dogmatism of the Party leaders forced them to distrust and suspect students, who are by nature interested in everything new and progressive. The Party apparatus considered students and teachers of the social sciences in particular as a priori infected with revisionism and other dangerous kinds of thinking. Students were forbidden to form organizations or clubs, and at the Philosophical Faculty* of Prague's Charles University repeated purges, expulsions and other punishments were administered.

It was an irony of fate that, when the students rebelled, they did so where the leaders least expected it—at the Prague Polytechnic Institute and in the natural sciences department at the Charles University. Their protest was entirely non-political, but the police brutally transformed it into a political event of tremendous importance.

In several new student hostels in the student dormitory complex at Strahov in Prague there had been repeated electricity failures. The causes were typical: several years before, someone —it was never publicly proven who—invented a method of "saving" the expensive non-ferrous metals used in the manufacture of electrical cables by using plastics instead. This innovation was generously rewarded, in spite of the fact that technicians protested: the plants were forced by Party fiat to put it into production. Some plasticized cables had been used for the electrical installations at the Strahov student hostels. Consequently, students often had no light to study by, and no heat. Repeated protests accomplished nothing. For more than a year the management of the hostels and the student committee wrote countless protests and requests for electrical repairs. But since the repairs were costly and required much work, there was no one to undertake them. Letters were not answered, promises were not kept.

* The liberal arts department, as opposed to the theoretical and applied science courses. Ed.

On the evening of October 30, 1967, the lights again went out and the radiators became cold. About two thousand students came out of the Strahov hostels carrying candles and shouting, "We want light!" Purely by chance, that same evening the Central Committee of the Party was meeting at the Hradčany Castle, which rises above the Strahov quarter. The meeting had not been publicly announced, and no one except the highest Party people and the police knew about it. When the student protesters, chanting their subversive slogan "We want light!" came near the castle (there was no other way for them to get to the center of the city), the police, who thought this was a demonstration against the Central Committee, struck with exceptional brutality. Students were dispersed with truncheons and pursued into their rooms in the hostels, where tear gas was used. Several students had to be hospitalized; many received first aid. News of the police action spread like lightning. The official press justified the police by writing about the anti-socialist aims of the students who had been encouraged by writers.

Thus three streams of opposition—economic stagnation, nationalist grievances and the suppressed rights of citizens—swelled to one main stream whose force surprised the Party leadership. Because the torrent had been building for years in the latent energy of new thought among intellectuals, it found expression at the highest level: in the Central Committee of the Communist Party. Surprisingly, Novotný was unseated by the same Central Committee whose members only thirty months before had been hand-picked by him for their devotion and loyalty. The sense that the country was on the verge of disaster, and the arbitrariness of their chief, forced even these people to rebel.

In this way the stage was set for January 1968, for what history would call the Czechoslovak Spring, which subsequently influenced the world political situation and which has been called the last chance of the world Communist movement.

Chapter **5**

Change in the Central Committee

Ever since 1948 the Communist Party of Czechoslovakia had been struggling with the problem of who held power in the country. Who really governed—the Central Committee of the Party through the Presidium, or the government? Socially, the Party was the country's leading institution, and its predominant role was even written into the new constitution of 1960, which an obedient parliament passed at Novotný's request. If, however, the Party governed, what about the constitutional bodies, parliament and the government? Were they merely executive instruments; according to Stalinist theory a kind of conveyor belt? Did they exist only to execute whatever the Presidium decided? Or should they, especially the government, govern? Wouldn't two centers of power create needless duplication?

In 1951, while the trial of Rudolf Slánský (then General Secretary of the Party) was being prepared, Klement Gottwald, leader of the Party and President of the Republic, asked rhetorically in a speech: Where is Czechoslovakia's real government, in the Central Committee building near Prašná brána or at the Strahov Academy, which since 1945 had been the seat of the government?* In a reply that was also an accusation of Slánský,

---

* Prašná brána is a fifteenth-century powder tower set astride one of the main boulevards of central Prague; the Strahov Academy, once a student refectory and before that a convent, is set on Prague's highest hill behind Hradčany Castle. Ed.

Gottwald answered unequivocally that, as General Secretary of the Party he [Slánský] had arrogated too much power, that, while the Central Committee should direct the state politically without exercising administrative powers, the government should govern.

The original dilemma, however, remained unresolved: the centralized system and the dictatorship of the Party led inevitably to a concentration of actual power in the hands of the Party leadership. Novotný, the First Secretary of the Party, was elected President of the Republic; with other members of the Party nominated as leading functionaries of the government, the center of power unquestionably shifted to the Party's supreme instrument, the Presidium.

This created an untenable duplication of power: two centralized bureaucracies, the government and the Party. Each was in the other's way; sometimes they competed, at other times they put obstacles in each other's way. But as time passed, the Party's bureaucratic system began to take precedence over the government's. Because all state power was concentrated in the hands of the Party Presidium, each Ministry had a corresponding department within the apparatus of the Central Committee to direct the work of that Ministry. The same situation of redundant bureaucracies developed in the districts and provinces.

Finally, the Ministry official, who was obliged to consult his opposite number in the Central Committee apparatus on the most trivial question, concluded that he need not ask his superior in the Ministry, not even the Minister himself; then he concluded that he need not decide anything for himself, because the official of the Party apparatus would eventually decide. The government, on which responsibility for the whole social system lay, thus became, in reality, a screen behind which some person who had no legal right to make decisions had the last word; what is more, that person acted autonomously. On the other hand, instead of concerning itself with politics or taking care of its real work (which, after all, was to lead the whole of society toward socialism), the Party apparatus was making countless organizational, administrative and economic decisions—anonymously, with no legal basis and, naturally, inexpertly. The upshot was universal irresponsibility, universal anonymity; another result was the political sterility of the Communist Party and the apathy of its members.

In 1963 it was decided that advisory committees to the Party's Central Committee be created, composed of experts from the scientific institutes, governmental departments and the Party apparatus. These groups would study new problems arising in society and present their results to the Party leadership, together with concrete proposals. It was a good plan—to surround the people in whose hands power lay with a kind of scientific brain trust—but it soon clashed with the self-interest and self-importance of leading politicians, above all, Novotný. Lawyers, historians, sociologists and economists worked out memoranda containing theoretical analyses and concrete proposals. In passing through the Party apparatus, however, these memoranda were arbitrarily changed before they reached the hands of the members of the Presidium. Even in their groomed, pruned form most of the memoranda angered Novotný, who found in them "bourgeois nationalism," "bourgeois democratism," "revisionism" and "intellectual radicalism," and either threw them into the wastepaper basket or worked them over so diligently that nothing remained of the original thoughts and proposals.

Members of these commissions had been thinking since 1966 about the progressive decay of the whole system, and above all about the fact that the Party was supplanting the government and leading the whole society into a blind alley. After lengthy discussions, proposals were put forward: it was euphemistically noted that they might lead to "the separation of church and state," i.e. of the Party and the government, which would guarantee the constitutional institutions a chance to govern and allow the Party to fulfill its political and ideological function. These proposals, considerably cut and disfigured by the Party apparatus, yet attempting at least partial amelioration, were to be discussed by the plenum of the Central Committee in October 1967.

Meanwhile, however, all conflicts grew sharper as the Writers' Congress approached.

At the plenum of the Central Committee in September, Novotný and Hendrych announced tougher policies and inaugurated repressions of the intelligentsia. Novotný's coarseness augmented the Slovaks' feelings of injury. The screws were tightened once more; again a moderate thaw was followed by a hard frost.

When the plenum of the Central Committee assembled in October to discuss proposals (which had already been published) about the position of the Party and its work, Novotný announced that these proposals were not to be discussed. In their place an insignificant, empty review of economic problems was substituted.

At this point the obedient committee members, all personally chosen by Novotný at the Thirteenth Congress, revolted. One after another, they asked to take part in the discussion; then, instead of talking about economic problems, they protested the fact that they were not discussing the published proposals. Criticisms of Novotný's arbitrary behavior and peremptory methods followed. Speakers emphasized that the conflicts were increasing, that no one was solving them, that apathy had overcome the workers, that the Party had ceased to be a political party and become a substitute for the administrative apparatus.

And then Mrs. Mária Sedláková rose. A Slovak, a former textile worker, an old Communist who took part in the Slovak national uprising of 1944, she worked in the Bratislava editorial office of *Pravda,* the mouthpiece of the Slovak Party. She was known for her sincerity, her loyalty to the Party and also for her feminine (perhaps a shade sentimental, yet open and courageous) manner. She admonished Novotný for offensive behavior during his journey through Slovakia.

She was followed by the First Secretary of the Party in Slovakia, Alexander Dubček. In Bratislava he had refused to take reprisals against the writers, as Novotný had done in

Prague. Dubček presented a number of Slovak complaints. He spoke not only about the insult to Slovak national consciousness but also about Slovak autonomy and how it had been reduced, contrary to the professed aims of the Party and the government's program. Prague's centralism had made the Slovak constitutional institutions puppets, he protested, and Bratislava was deprived even of the status of the capital city of Slovakia.

Sharply countering these criticisms, the enraged Novotný replied. He spoke of revisionism and radicalism and unceremoniously accused Dubček and other Slovaks of bourgeois nationalism. In the fifties such accusations would have meant a long prison sentence; now, with the thaw ended and the frost begun again, such political trials might be repeated, especially since justice and the state security and police apparatus were arbitrarily controlled by Antonín Novotný himself, helped by the head of the so-called Eighth Department of the Central Committee of the Party, a certain Miroslav Mamula. Not even other members of the Presidium were allowed to interfere where security and justice were concerned.

The plenum dispersed in this atmosphere and under the shadow of the brutal police attack on the demonstrating students. The leading politicians departed for Moscow for celebrations of the fiftieth anniversary of the October Revolution. Before leaving, Novotný offered Dubček a place in the delegation. Dubček refused. In his place, representing the Slovaks, went Michal Chudík, Chairman of the puppet Slovak National Council and a faithful servant of Novotný. The delegation stayed in Moscow for more than fourteen days. This was Novotný's tactical error.

His opponents used his absence to mobilize the Party functionaries against him. Almost to a man the Slovaks stood against Novotný, united mainly by the national question. Mamula, alerted that something was brewing in Slovakia, sent his security agents (so the rumors ran in Prague) to follow Dubček and other "bourgeois nationalists" and, if necessary, to take steps against them. In Bratislava, however, the First Secretary of the Communist

Party of Slovakia had his own security men. So it happened that one set of hounds was followed by another, and each security group effectively paralyzed the other.

The Moravian districts too joined the opposition to Novotný. The uncertain future of the Ostrava coal and metallurgical industry, menaced as it was by proposed structural changes in the economy, played an important role here. Brno, the second Moravian district, also had reason to protest the accentuated centralism of Prague. The eastern part of Bohemia, around Hradec-Králové, became disaffected, too. Finally the delegations of six districts (that is, the majority, for counting the Prague delegation there were eleven) united in opposition to Novotný.

In the last half of December 1967, the plenum of the Central Committee was again called together to complete its analysis of the place and role of the Party. Rumors were widespread that a confrontation would take place at this session; the atmosphere grew tense. The army was preparing for maneuvers, allegedly within its normal training program, but the sudden call-up of numerous reservists gave substance to whispers that a *coup d'état* was in the offing.

To his great surprise, on returning from Moscow Antonín Novotný found opposition to himself even within the Presidium. Hitherto faithful and obedient colleagues opposed him—and he called Brezhnev in Moscow for help.

Brezhnev came in person. Individual members of the Presidium, greatly displeased and surprised, were called to discussions with the Soviet guest, who, naturally, always referred to the Soviet principle of non-interference in the internal affairs of fraternal parties—yet praised Novotný, emphasizing his great statesmanship and international significance.

The Czechs and Slovaks presented to their Soviet guest memorable examples of Novotný's working methods, declaring that problems had developed because of rather than in spite of these methods. They pointed out the impossibility of further collaboration with a man who concentrated far too much power in his own hands and misused it in a way that was leading the country to disaster. Brezhnev listened to everything, obviously grasped the fact that the opposition was more serious than he had thought, and realized the impossibility of defending his protégé. According to the accounts of some who participated in these discussions, Brezhnev counseled prudence and calmness and departed with the words, *"Eto vaše dĕlo"*—"It's your own affair."

Late in December, the plenum of the Central Committee met, and the revolt against Novotný broke out openly. One after another, the members of the Central Committee stood to accuse the First Secretary of willfulness, subjectivism, uncomradely behavior and harsh treatment of subordinates and colleagues. They protested not only the personal qualities of the First Secretary, but also the whole policy of the Party as he had directed it; the state had been brought to near catastrophe by a personal regime of dogmatic Stalinism. Again and again misdeeds and injustices committed against the Slovaks were cited. Members spoke of the dangerous discord between the intellectuals and the workers, deepened by the demagogy that was the First Secretary's favorite weapon; of half-hearted economic reforms that had led the country into a cul-de-sac; of the apathy of the entire Party; of the decline in efficiency and responsibility of the state apparatus. The Novotný regime was accused of creating a universal dislike for the Party and a distaste for socialism generally among the young. Finally there was a demand that Novotný resign the leadership of the Party and step down as First Secretary.

Novotný and his most faithful followers defended themselves stubbornly. They insisted that the First Secretary had always acted in accord with his fellow members who until now had never expressed disagreement with him. They denied the existence of conflicts in Czechoslovak society, or attempted to blame them on imperialistic intrigues. They bitterly attacked the academician Ota Šik, who again pointed out that economic reform could not succeed without a thorough democratization of the Party and the whole society. The conservatives accused Šik of trying to solve economic problems by lowering the workers' standard of living and by mass unemployment.

Above all, they maneuvered and attempted to defend Novotný's position. They wanted to postpone discussing a separation of the functions of the First Secretary from those of the President until after the elections. By then a new President would be chosen and Novotný would be better able to continue as First Secretary. They demanded that the decision be postponed at least until after the international meeting of Communist Parties in Budapest in February, so that Novotný's international prestige might be salvaged. The Foreign Minister, Václav David, a champion of the President, capped the argument by pointing out that the imperialist press too had attacked Novotný, and that to deprive him of office now would confirm reports of their differences that had appeared in the capitalist press.

The highlight of the discussion was the stand taken by some of Novotný's hitherto most loyal friends, climaxed by the appearance of Jiří Hendrych, who excused his own severe attack upon the writers by stating that Novotný had forced him to make it.

So the state and Party crisis reached a peak, which was concealed in the Czech and Slovak nations, whose information media were not allowed to release one word about these events. Naturally, the foreign correspondents who came to Prague in great numbers were able to gather reliable information and fully inform the world at large. Resolution of the crisis was, in the meantime, postponed for trivial reasons. Christmas was approaching; on Christmas Eve in Czechoslovakia each family lights candles on the tree, the children receive gifts and the whole family gathers at the festive table to eat fried carp. While the Central Committee sat and debated the fate of the Party and the state, the members' discontented wives telephoned: when would they finish? The traditional Christmas Eve was more important than any politics. So as not to break the Christmas tradition, the December Central Committee meeting was interrupted. It was decided to continue the session on January 3, when the Presidium, enlarged by delegates from the districts—

two representatives from each—must definitely resolve the question of division of functions between First Secretary and President, if necessary by suggesting a new candidate to the plenum.

The Christmas carp was consumed in peace and the children received their gifts while the wildest rumors circulated among the people. The President, Antonín Novotný, delivered his traditional January 1 pronouncement, as colorless and empty of content as ever.

When, on January 3, he did not summon the enlarged Presidium, the supplementary delegates forced the convocation of the Presidium on January 4 and a session of the plenum of the Central Committee for the same day. The passionate discussion began once again with mutual attacks and maneuvers. At the end, Novotný had to stand before the plenum and ask to be relieved of the duties of First Secretary. His resignation was accepted by all the members present, with one exception. Behind the scenes, the fight over his successor began. Because the Presidium and the district delegates could not agree on a choice between the two obvious candidates—the then Premier, a Slovak, Josef Lenárt and Oldřich Černík, a member of the Presidium —a compromise was found. Alexander Dubček, who had been First Secretary of the Communist Party of Slovakia, was elected First Secretary of the Communist Party of Czechoslovakia at noon on Saturday, January 6.

Chapter 6

Winter Intermezzo

The new men did not even attempt to take power immediately. Alexander Dubček returned to his family in Bratislava. All Slovakia celebrated "our man's" victory; the following day, Sunday, Dubček went to a football match and the spectators gave him a prolonged ovation.

For the time being Novotný accepted defeat. It was discovered later that some of his supporters and protégés on the General Staff were preparing a military putsch. The preparations so lacked finesse, however, that even in embryo they came to nothing, and there is no evidence that Novotný's partisans acted with the knowledge of their protector.

One cannot reproach the principal actors in this drama for not realizing at the time what they had begun. The initiators and directors of important historical events almost never know the direction their innovations will take and cannot foresee the implications of their actions. But an experienced observer could not doubt what was happening. For the first time in forty years, the leadership of the Communist Party of Czechoslovakia had been changed after a discussion lasting several months in which all the democratic rules of discourse had been preserved. For the first time in any country in which Communists held power, the first man of the Party was deposed without becoming an "unperson." Novotný was ousted without accusations of treachery, without being arrested or having his telephone cut, without disappearing through the trap door of history. On the contrary, Novotný remained President of the Republic.

Even more startling, after the meeting, the Central Committee's communiqué announced that the division of functions had come about "in accordance with the inauguration of the democratic process," and that the dismissal of Novotný from the functions of First Secretary "would increase the significance of the President as a symbol of the socialist power of the working class." The Committee also thanked Novotný for his "meritorious and sacrificing work" and for "the outstanding successes that the Party achieved in the country and in the international Communist movement, all of which were connected with his personality." This too had never happened in any Communist Party change of leadership.

At the same time the Central Committee voted to classify the entire December and January discussions. The minutes— over a thousand pages since more than 150 speakers took part —would be available only to the highest functionaries of the Party. Yet the world press was carrying detailed information about what was happening in the Spanish Hall of Prague's Hradčany Castle, where the Central Committee was sitting. Commentators spoke of the meeting as an historical event, but the Czechoslovak press was not allowed to comment on it. A few days after the end of the January session of the plenum, Jiří Hendrych, who remained the ideological secretary, called together the chief editors of Prague newspapers to tell them that nothing had really happened, that the division of functions was only a measure to improve the work of the Presidium and the Party apparatus. He was especially adamant that the press must not in any way emphasize national conflicts or imply that the end of Novotný's regime of personal power was an important step toward a truly democratic society.

Official attempts to pretend that nothing had changed failed, however. Members of the Central Committee and the Party apparatus who were present at the sessions spread the news by word of mouth. Comments by the world press and radio penetrated to the Czechoslovak people. The censors, who had a premonition that the end of their misrule was approaching, relaxed their vigilance. Articles began to appear first in *Kulturný život,* the weekly periodical of the Slovak writers, then, timidly, in other newspapers, expressing the opinion that the leading role of the Communist Party could not be secured by decrees alone, but must be daily defended and legitimized. Some articles suggested that the Party apparatus must not interfere in the functions of the government or take its place. Citizens of a socialist state had a right to be informed about the actions of the highest bodies of the state, they said, and the full rehabilitation of victims of the fifties' political trials must begin.

The first important article was written by Josef Smrkovský, then Minister of Forests and Waterways, who was one of the leaders of the opposition to Novotný; it appeared on January 21 in the trade union daily, *Práce.* Other articles followed early in February in the Party paper, *Rudé právo.* The secretary of the law commission of the Central Committee, Zdeněk Mlynář, wrote in *Rudé právo* on February 13 that it was not a question of perfecting the present system, but rather of fundamentally reforming the whole structure of power, exactly as economic reform should change the structure of the Czechoslovak economy. In a televised interview, Professor Goldstuecker, the new chairman of the Writers' Union, demanded that reprisals against the writers' weekly be revoked and the expelled writers reinstated in the Party.

Alexander Dubček delivered his maiden speech as First Secretary before the Agricultural Congress at the beginning of February. Talking of the democratization of the whole system, he pointed out that workers in agricultural cooperatives had been systematically underestimated during former regimes; now they were to become equal partners with workers and intellectuals, enjoying full democratic rights in the society.

These modest speeches and first signs of a new course aroused immense public interest. Accustomed to apathy and to political indifference, the people wakened to unheard-of political activity. But only Antonín Novotný's attempt to mount a counteroffensive started the chain reaction that brought the full participation of the people, although the scandal surrounding the departure of General Jan Šejna also caused an explosion.

In the middle of February, Novotný—while still a member of the Party Presidium and President of the Republic—visited the biggest factory in Prague to deliver a speech to the assembled workers in which he attempted to rehabilitate himself. In a demagogic manner, Novotný attacked the progressive wing of the Central Committee, especially Šik and the rest of the reformers, declaring that they were trying to solve economic difficulties at the workers' expense. They were trying to lower the standard of living, and mass unemployment would follow their reforms, he said.

This forced the principal representatives of the opposition into the open. One after another they came to public meetings to repeat at large what they had previously said only behind the closed doors of the Spanish Hall.

February 25 was the twentieth anniversary of the Communist Party's coming to power, and leaders of all the socialist states were gathered in Prague. At the inaugural celebration all but one of the foreign guests hailed the rejuvenating process that had begun in January and spoke of the need for democratization. Only Gomułka, the Polish leader, thought it unnecessary to acknowledge the reforms by so much as a word. As President of the Republic, Novotný spoke in his usual manner at the festive parade of the Army and the Workers' Militia in the Old Town Square. After him, Alexander Dubček spoke once more about the democratization of the whole Czechoslovak society.

Afterward all the leaders, including Dubček, departed for Sofia for the meeting of the Political Committee of the Warsaw Pact states. The following day the news about General Jan Šejna broke. On the evening of February 27, the Czechoslovak radio announced that the Presidium of the National Assembly had agreed to the State Procurator's request that Jan Šejna, vice-chairman of the National Assembly, be deprived of his immunity, and a warrant for his arrest had been issued.

Šejna had entered the army after February 1948. His working-class origin and membership in the Communist Party guaranteed him swift advancement and a successful career. Recently he had become first secretary of the Party committee in the Ministry of National Defense, and been promoted to general by Novotný. Šejna's new position gave him immense power, together with access to all top-secret military and personal files. He became Novotný's personal protégé and an intimate friend of his son.

Now all the details of the *dolce vita* of this staunch Communist, a pillar of the Communist establishment, were revealed. With the help of Colonel Jaroslav Moravec, his aide-de-camp (who was also detained), Šejna had carried on illegal dealings in clover seed cultivated on army farms, selling this expensive commodity to the agricultural cooperative in his own electoral district and pocketing the money. Abusing his friendship with the President's son, Šejna had also speculated in foreign cars. He had deserted his wife and caroused in Prague night clubs with a series of mistresses. A luxurious summer residence had been built for him by soldiers, who worked without pay, out of materials belonging to the Army.

But General Šejna also had far-reaching political ambitions. During the December session of the Central Committee, the General Staff, too, was meeting. General Václav Prchlík, head of the army's principal political department, put forward the opinion that, in view of the uncertain situation in the Central Committee, the Army must obey only the orders of its supreme commander, President Novotný, providing his orders were also signed by the remaining members of the Party Presidium. The secretary of the political committee in the Ministry of Defense regarded this opinion as mutinous. During the January Central Committee session at which Novotný's fate was decided, the General Staff once again met. General Šejna, over General Martin Dzúr's opposition, succeeded in sending a letter in the name of the General Staff to the Central Committee, demanding the retention of Novotný as Secretary. The commander of the tank detachments, General Janko, at his friend General Šejna's behest, ordered the tank brigade in Tábor to move immediately toward Prague. Hearing of this, General Prchlík cancelled Janko's order. The tank brigade remained halfway between Prague and Tábor, then returned to its headquarters. The letter was delivered to the Central Committee after the vote that deprived Novotný of the First Secretaryship.

So the attempt at a putsch organized by General Šejna misfired. When he heard from his friends in the police that an investigation of the clover-seed affair had started, he realized that his chief protector no longer had power to shield him, and he decided to escape. The day after he lost his parliamentary immunity, it was announced that General Šejna, accompanied by his twenty-year-old mistress and his son, had crossed the frontier into Hungary.

Everyone was sure that the general was making for Albania. Where else could he go, this steadfast supporter of the dictatorship of the proletariat, this opponent of revisionist intellectuals, this protégé of Antonín Novotný?

But Jan Šejna did not go to Albania. Indeed, what would he have done there? It would have meant, at the least, the end of the *dolce vita*. The general crossed the frontier from Yugoslavia into Italy. In Rome he was received by members of the American Embassy and put on a plane for Washington, together with his mistress and son. There he began to tell eager listeners in the CIA all he knew about the military secrets of the Warsaw Pact, and, more important, all he knew about the personal characteristics of the Czechoslovak and Warsaw Pact general staffs, including which general was devoted to alcohol and which to women. It is hardly surprising that the CIA investigated Šejna for several months and that he then received political asylum, including a comfortable dwelling, a car, prospects of writing a film script and so on. After all, a prosperous America knows how to reward services rendered much more generously than does a dictatorship of the proletariat.

The Šejna revelations ruffled the relatively calm surface of public opinion in Czechoslovakia. The regime that had introduced a leveling of wages with the argument that everyone had the same stomach, the regime that boasted of the Spartan modesty and abstemiousness of its representatives, had bred a man who spoke hypocritically of socialism and equality, who stormed against rewards to writers and artists while he devoted his own life to pleasures. The staunch bolshevik who at meetings thundered against the imperialistic diversions of intellectuals had deserted to America the moment his misdeeds were uncovered. The workers were furious.

Purely by chance, censorship was abolished just as the Šejna affair broke. Even this had a grotesque aspect. Protests against censorship were made at several plenums of the Central Committee. In Party circles there was talk of doing away with it, especially among those preparing the new Action Program. Meanwhile, the old secret directive stood. Promulgated by Novotný in 1966, it gave the censor the right to interfere arbitrarily, without restriction, to protect the interests of the Party and the state.

The ideological secretary, Jiří Hendrych, who carried out the reprisals against the Writers' Congress and who had deserted Novotný at the plenum of the Central Committee, joined the opposition and stated that he had been forced to act against the writers. Now he negotiated with the representatives of the Writers' Union about the renewal of their literary weekly. In order to save his own and the Party's prestige, Hendrych imposed one condition: the new weekly must change its name from *Literární noviny* (Literary News) to *Literární listy* (Literary Pages). He must have known that the writers who, even before, had not allowed themselves to be muzzled and who had courageously stood against the regime of personal power would now, as victors, be yet more vocal. He must have expected that, as they had previously fought censorship, they would now do so even more skillfully. Yet what would happen to Hendrych's recently achieved fame as a liberal, for which he had betrayed Novotný, were he forced to reinstate censorship?

In order to save his reputation, to avoid being once again identified as the main obscurantist of Communism, he proposed to the Presidium that censorship be abolished by March 1. The Presidium was already thinking along these lines. (The first number of *Literární listy* was to appear on March 1.) His proposal was accepted. The old secret directive of 1966 was annulled just as alert journalists received full news of the Šejna affair, of the prepared military putsch, of the foreign car dealings of President Novotný's son, of the building of summer residences, and, above all, of President Novotný's direct responsibility for General Šejna's career.

Chapter **7**

Revolution through Words

The first shot in the controversy over Novotný's direct responsibility for the Šejna affair was fired by the trade union daily, *Práce*. It echoed through all of Czechoslovakia. Frightened Party bureaucrats telephoned Dubček in Sofia. Dubček, in turn, telephoned the editor of *Práce* in Prague, pleading for moderation.

But it was useless. After *Práce* came other dailies, weeklies, the radio and television. There was freedom of the press and other communications media such as Czechoslovakia had not known for twenty years.

Dailies that for years had been dull, gray and almost identical in content suddenly revealed unexpected color, vitality and variety. The political weeklies published essays, stories and commentaries, round-table discussions on political, economic and cultural themes. Radio discussions and commentaries attracted millions of listeners, and television introduced subjects that for a long time had been considered taboo.

For some years the Socialist Academy—an organization for public education—had organized symposia on various themes. Anyone could attend these and hear groups of experts reply to set questions. In early spring 1968 such an evening of questions and answers was arranged in one of Prague's biggest halls with Josef Smrkovský as one of the experts. Rehabilitated politicians from the period of the fifties trials were also to appear on the panel, among them some popular writers, as well as Marie Švermová, a former Party Secretary who had spent eight years in prison, and Josef Hejzlar, the former chairman of the Youth Organization. This evening, at which the crimes and faults of the Novotný regime were quite openly discussed, attracted such a crowd that several thousand people could not get into the hall. By gathering outside the auditorium, the overflow crowd brought traffic to a standstill. It was decided to continue the session the following week in the central hall where huge commercial exhibitions were held. On the second evening twenty thousand young people came and followed the debates in a most disciplined manner from seven o'clock in the evening until two o'clock in the morning. The proceedings were broadcast and millions of listeners heard a discussion distinguished by humor, audacity, and above all by various interpretations of socialism, of the meaning of Czechoslovakia's alliance with the Soviet Union, and of the new (and until then completely untried) democratic model of socialism.

The greatest shock to the whole nation, especially to Party members, was the revelation of the political trials of the fifties. Only one of these trials had been public, that of Rudolf Slánský, then First Secretary of the Party, and thirteen others accused along with him. Other trials, in which tens of thousands of people were condemned to death or to long years of imprisonment, had been secret. Czechoslovakia, of all the socialist countries, was the most affected by such trials in spite of (or perhaps because of) the fact that, among these countries, she had the deepest democratic traditions. Only a small circle of people knew the truth about these trials and even they knew only part of it.

That truth compromised the existing leadership of the Czechoslovak Communist Party and especially its leader at that time, Klement Gottwald, who had died in March 1953, within days of Stalin's death. Gottwald was a popular leader of the workers and had for some time been head of the Party, which was the only Communist Party in Central Europe that was a legal party with a mass following. He was Prime Minister when the Communists took power in 1948. After Eduard Beneš' resignation, Gottwald also became President of Czechoslovakia. In previous years he had been an original thinker compared to other prominent Communists: he was a good popular speaker and it was he who, after the Liberation in 1945, had been most articulate about a specific Czechoslovak road to socialism. Unlike Yugoslavia's Tito, however, Gottwald had lived many years in Moscow as an émigré. Subjectively, he had absorbed the atmosphere of Byzantine and bureaucratic self-will that reigned there. He was too loyal to Stalin to set himself up, like Tito, against Stalinism in order to outline a specifically Czechoslovak course.

In the end, Gottwald succumbed to pressure, and by his own hand initiated terrorist methods of government, sacrificing his best colleagues and personal friends with whom he had shared years of political work. Thousands of Czechoslovakia's most able politicians and economists were caught up in the political terror and the police rule aided by Soviet security experts that followed. Blindly, the whole country imitated Soviet methods evolved for a different country with a different social structure, different traditions and a different mentality. Gottwald himself fell victim to these years of terror. Realizing his responsibility and weakness, in his last years he broke down completely and became an alcoholic. Four months after Gottwald sent his best friend Slánský to the gallows, he died.

Now the daily press began to publish accounts of the crimes committed by the secret police in the era of the political trials. The public knew the facts about the old Communists who had become the victims of juridical crimes, but the terrible tortures, the sadistic treatment of prisoners and the complete denial of human dignity entailed were unknown. Now one exposé after another appeared about methods that had been used in examining prisoners. Even more, for the first time the public learned of the treatment meted out to tens of thousands of anti-fascist fighters, to participants in the war against Nazism on the Western and Eastern fronts, and to former inmates of German concentration camps. Unlawfully, thousands of officers of the Czechoslovak Army were held without formal indictment in concentration camps and tortured. The names of some torturers became known; quite a few had learned their trade under the Nazis, in whose service they had performed the same function as lately under a socialist regime. Television arranged confrontations between former political prisoners and their torturers from the secret police or prison staffs. These confrontations shook the conscience of hundreds of thousands of viewers who were often unable to believe that such things were possible. The radio broadcast a program called "Songs by Telephone" during which a radio commentator telephoned people accused of different crimes, or of blindly following Novotný, and asked them to justify their actions, then played them a song chosen in order to expose them to ridicule.

For the first time, the communications media were able to go behind the scenes and carry their own reports of the district and regional Party conferences taking place that March. For the first time, the public got regular news of discussions in the Presidium or the government. This was the end of politics behind closed doors, where matters were decided in the name of the people, and supposedly for them, without their knowledge. The public now could follow and in part control the behavior and actions of the various, often self-promoted leaders of the people.

This information explosion, an unfamiliar free discussion of fundamental social problems, caused unusual public activity. Public affairs actually became a matter of concern to everyone. In all places of work there were discussions about the previous night's television and radio programs, about the points raised by this or that commentator, or about the articles of well-known journalists and scientists. For many years people had been accustomed to buying one paper, which the majority of them read backwards from the sports page. Now everyone bought several newspapers because something different and interesting was to be found in each of them, and papers were read straight through.

People complained that there was not enough time to read everything that interested them. Editorial offices were flooded with complaints that radio and television broadcast major news programs simultaneously so that people had to choose between them when they would have preferred to follow both. Circulation of dailies and weeklies rose astronomically, checked only by the lack of newsprint and the capacity of the printing presses. For the better-known weeklies such as *Literární listy* and *Reportér,* long queues formed at the newsstands and whole issues were sold out immediately.

The press, radio and television brought the people to a full realization of what had happened in January and what the Party apparatus had tried to conceal. The communications media ended the political career of more than one "statesman" invited before the television cameras, where under pitiless lights and the probing questions of the commentators, his inner poverty was revealed. There were round-table discussions about all the problems of public life. Discussion of the insufficiencies and mistakes of the regime and of the plans for reform in political, economic and cultural spheres uncovered taboos, presenting all the problems of socialism to the mass of readers, viewers and listeners. The uncovering of terrible crimes helped to pillory the hypocrisy of those who, hiding behind noble phrases, had been politically responsible. At the same time, the media performed a human service in the education of the people, who realized that their own indifference had made them jointly responsible for these crimes.

If the events of the Czechoslovak Spring of 1968 were a revolution, it was perhaps the first revolution in human history in which the chief weapons were words, not guns. The communications media were the main vehicle of the revolution. One could only admire the journalists who for twenty years had been taught to be the megaphones of leading politicians. After twenty years of not being able to write from their own convictions but being forced to write according to the Party's latest pronouncement (in whose composition they had no part), these journalists soon found their own voices and the courage to fight for their own truth. They quickly learned what for twenty years they had systematically had to unlearn—the art of polemic, of discussion, of defending their own opinions.

A large part in this explosion of journalistic freedom was played by two decades' accumulated longing to be allowed to say what one really thought regardless of the political consequences, or of the fact that a small nation on the very frontier of the European world must realistically consider its own position. The heady possibility of using the freedom of the press so suddenly achieved understandably led to extremes and to radical viewpoints.

Every journalist, every journalistic scribe, had a chance to publish or to broadcast anything he wanted to. Normally, every newspaper office, radio or television station has its own sponsoring organization and editors in chief, who set policy and decide what is and is not to be printed or broadcast. During the Czechoslovak Spring these regulating factors ceased to exist. The publishers, i.e. societies or political parties who, according to the law, were allowed to publish newspapers, had been only fictitious because the ideological content of publications was decided by the central apparatus of the Communist Party. In the chaos after January 1968, this apparatus, uncertain about its own future and its own rights, had ceased to function. Thus it was possible for the trade union press, *Práce* especially, to inaugurate a successful campaign against its own publisher; the union leadership (which was in the hands of Novotný's men) was forced to leave public life. The same thing happened at *Lidová demokracie,* the paper of the People's Party; consequently the hirelings of the former President, Father Josef Plojhar in particular, were forced to leave. Similarly, the editors in chief ceased to function, the majority of them being men without the simplest journalistic skills but faithful executors of orders from above. They were not dismissed; they continued to draw salaries and to sit in their offices where, confused by what was happening, afraid of losing their careers and their livelihood, they stopped directing editorial policy. As no more orders descended from above and censorship had ceased, they allowed anything written by their staff members to appear in print or on the air.

Extreme, ill-considered, half-baked opinions thus could—and did—appear in the pages of the newspapers. Some articles asked for the neutrality of Czechoslovakia—without taking into account the complexity of the international situation and the balance of forces in both European camps, especially the delicate balance of power that such a step would immediately upset with catastrophic results for world peace and for Czechoslovakia's international position. Revelations of the crimes of the political police during the trials of the fifties had brought to the surface questions about the Soviet advisers, their function in Czechoslovakia and their contribution to the witch hunt. The blind imitation of Soviet economic models that had brought about the crisis in the Czechoslovak economy was also questioned. All this led to articles demanding a definite separation from the Soviet Union. The authors of such articles never considered—and when it was brought to their attention only shrugged their shoulders—that in Moscow such opinions would be taken as proof of the imminent danger that Czechoslovakia would leave the socialist camp.

Other essays and commentaries suggested that the democratization stressed by the new Party leadership should eventually become a real democracy, which presupposes a plurality of political parties, truly free elections and the existence of an opposition in the form of one or more opposition parties. Once again, the authors of such ideas refused to consider the fact that the ruling Communist Party would not voluntarily surrender power. The revelation of past crimes and mistakes had very seriously shaken its position. In such a situation, for the Party to tolerate a political opposition would mean political suicide and a surrender of power by the Communists. This in turn would lead to immense domestic and international complications whose consequences would be difficult to forecast.

There was also the campaign started by the philosopher Ivan

Sviták of Prague's Charles University in the newspaper *Student*. Taking conjectures from an essay by an obscure émigré journalist about the circumstances of the 1948 death of Jan Masaryk, he demanded an investigation. Twenty years of silence about the significance and role of Tomáš G. Masaryk, the founder of the independent Czechoslovak state, and stupid attacks against his person—which was enshrined in the hearts of the people—had prepared the soil for a revival of the cult of the first Czechoslovak President. The relaxation of secret police terror had made possible open demonstrations honoring his memory; on March 7, Masaryk's birthday, a crowd went openly for the first time to the cemetery at Lány near Prague, to lay flowers on his grave and that of his son. Students turned this pilgrimage into a political demonstration. In this atmosphere Sviták's article forced the public prosecutor to open an investigation into the death of Jan Masaryk even though, after twenty years, it was doubtful that the investigation would find definitive proof of whether the official version of suicide was true, or whether Masaryk had been murdered. This inquiry, in the atmosphere of limitless and partly irresponsible freedom of the press, became an hysterical cause in the newspapers and on television. To it were added unsubstantiated rumors of the participation of "Beria's gorrillas" in the supposed crime—rumors impossible to prove. This provoked the first admonition of Czechoslovakia in the Soviet press.

In normal circumstances such excesses in the communications media would have been ephemeral phenomena. But circumstances in 1968 were far from normal. Voltaire once said to an opponent that though he detested his opinions, he would defend to the death his right to hold them. Only opponents of the Czechoslovak Spring were unwilling to defend one's right to an opinion. They on the contrary saw this right as proof of rising counterrevolution.

Extreme, irresponsible voices in the Czechoslovak media were on the whole only isolated, sporadic instances. On the whole, Czechoslovak journalists showed an unusual sense of responsibility, statesman-like judgment and political wisdom. Few voices demanded the impossible or escaped into speculative contemplations that did not respect reality and did not consider politics as the art of the possible. The Czechoslovak communications media brought home to Czechs and Slovaks the realization of great historical change. They prevented a return to pre-January conditions, deepened the democratic process and constantly pushed the hesitant, irresolute Party leadership further along the road of fundamental reforms. Their actions proved once again the enormous power commentators wield in any highly sophisticated society.

Chapter **8**

New Men to the Fore

Under public pressure, Antonín Novotný had been forced to abdicate the presidency. For the second time since 1935, when T. G. Masaryk gave up the presidency because of his advanced age and Eduard Beneš was elected to succeed him after a fight against right-wing intrigues, the question of who should become head of state was widely debated.

The more radical supporters of reform put forward Josef Smrkovský. Young people and students agitated for Čestmír Císař, who had become immensely popular with the young after he was removed as Minister of Education some years earlier by Novotný because of his extreme liberalism and made Ambassador to Rumania. But the Central Committee of the Communist Party agreed to accept the candidacy of General Ludvík Svoboda.

Among intellectuals especially, there were fears that Svoboda would be a puppet in the hands of some adroit politician, because of his advanced age and the fact that he had stood aside from politics. In the event, however, the choice proved fortunate.

Ludvík Svoboda was a young lieutenant in the Austro-Hungarian Army when World War I broke out. Like many other Czech and Slovak patriots he refused to fight for the Austro-Hungarian Emperor; at the first opportunity he surrendered to the Russians, toward whom he, as a Slav, felt sympathy and affinity.

In 1917, after the February Revolution, a Czechoslovak Legion was formed in Russia and Ludvík Svoboda became an officer in it. After the creation of the Republic and a memorable anabasis across Siberia, where the Legion battled against opponents of the Russian Revolution, he returned home and became an officer in the new Czechoslovak Army. In 1938, in the hour of mortal danger to the Czechoslovak state, he attained the rank of lieutenant colonel. Svoboda was a good soldier and completely apolitical. When the Nazis occupied the Republic, Svoboda, expecting war, decided to leave the country in order to continue the fight for independence abroad. He left for Poland where a great number of exiled Czechoslovak officers had gathered. General Lev Prchala, who was to become commanding officer of the future Czechoslovak Army unit there, held the highest rank. In contrast to Svoboda, Prchala was a soldier with high political ambitions on the extreme right. After the collapse of Poland, Prchala left for England to lead the right-wing opposition to Beneš and his pro-Russian orientation. Svoboda, who after Prchala's departure was the senior officer, remained with his friends and was interned by the Soviets.

When Germany attacked the Soviet Union and in London Beneš and Jan Masaryk signed a Treaty of Friendship with the Soviets, a Czechoslovak Army unit came into existence in the Soviet Union. Ludvík Svoboda [now a general–Ed.] was chosen as its commanding officer. Because of his military qualities and political neutrality, he was a suitable candidate for this post, which had to be filled by a man equally acceptable to the Czechoslovaks in London, the Czechoslovak Communists in Moscow, and the Soviet authorities. The Czechoslovak Army detachment on the Eastern Front later grew into a brigade, and by the end of the war had become a corps.

Extremely strained relations between the Poles and the Soviets resulted in the evacuation to Iran of the far larger Polish Army then in the Soviet Union, during the most critical days of the Battle of Stalingrad. The Czechoslovak unit remained in the USSR and distinguished itself in battle. In spite of the fact that it was numerically insignificant in comparison to the huge

Soviet Army, its contrast to the Poles led the Soviet press to stress and commend its loyalty and courage. Its commanding officer, General Svoboda, was singled out for special praise and decorated with numerous Soviet orders: he received the title of Hero of the Soviet Union and returned home as commanding officer of the liberating army.

Svoboda became Minister of National Defense in the Czechoslovak government. In February 1948, during the struggle for power between the bourgeois democratic groups and the Communists, Svoboda was once again an apolitical general and as Defense Minister refused to engage the Army in this struggle. His neutrality played a significant part in the Communist victory. Under the slogan that the Army will not march against the people (and there is no doubt that at that time the wide masses of the Czech and Slovak people, especially the workers, supported the Communists), Svoboda was partly responsible for the fact that February 1948 was a bloodless revolution.

He remained Minister of National Defense until Dr. Alexei Čepička, an ambitious politician and son-in-law of President Gottwald, appeared on the scene. Čepička aimed high and misused his closeness to the ill and broken Gottwald. With Gottwald's blessing, Čepička went, in the summer of 1951, to negotiate with Stalin. He carried a request that Soviet instructors be sent to the Czechoslovak Army. This was during the Korean War, and Communist leaders expected a world war. Čepička returned with a letter from Stalin, saying that he could not fulfill the request for instructors because he mistrusted Svoboda.

There are many reasons for thinking that the letter was forged. But it served its purpose. Svoboda was dismissed from office and in his place was nominated—Čepička. A purge of the Army followed during which the majority of the existing officer corps disappeared, even those who had been decorated in the Soviet Union during World War II.

Svoboda was imprisoned for some weeks and interrogated because he supposedly had protected Western spies in the Army.

When he was released he was sent as a clerk to an agricultural cooperative not far from his native town of Třebíč.

The career of this honest soldier would have ended in rural obscurity had there been no Twentieth Congress of the Communist Party of the Soviet Union. There Čepička, the main bearer of the personality cult in Czechoslovakia, was stripped of all responsibilities. When Nikita Khrushchev (who had known Svoboda personally during the war) visited Czechoslovakia, he asked in a jovial way what his old friend was doing. This inquiry was sufficient reason for Svoboda, dressed in his general's uniform and wearing all his orders, to be transported from Třebíč to Prague, there to be rehabilitated.

Svoboda was assigned to the Army's Historical Institute, where he worked on the history of the units he had commanded during World War II. Later he was elected a member of the National Assembly. This was the man chosen to succeed to the office of President of the Republic after Novotný's abdication.

The rumors that Svoboda was too old and ill, that he was unable to take part in active politics and that he would become a puppet in the hands of wire-pulling politicians all proved to be unsubstantiated. On the contrary, Svoboda symbolized the Czechoslovak military tradition. He commanded the units that had helped to liberate the Republic from the Nazis and was a man of personal honesty and honor who himself had suffered innocently in the fifties. As such, he was received by the whole people as the personification of their national ambitions. He was as popular in Slovakia as he was in Bohemia—which had a special significance in view of Novotný's parochial anti-Slovak tirades.

In the critical days of the invasion of Czechoslovakia by the armies of five of the Warsaw Pact states, Svoboda proved his courage and strength. Although his age and lack of political experience had encouraged people to think of him as merely a tool in someone's hands, he proved that he knew how to stand firm under pressure. He refused to bow before force and to nominate a collaborationist government that would give the occupation the stamp of legality. He forced the Soviet leaders to deal with him as an equal. Thanks solely to his courage, the liberation of the imprisoned Czechoslovak leaders was secured and some kind of compromise arrived at in Moscow.

Alexander Dubček was a completely different kind of man. He was meant to become the absolutely ordinary representative of the bureaucratic system of a Communist state (known the world over by the Russian name, *apparatchik*). He became instead, owing to a chance of history but also to his personal qualities, a world-wide symbol of democratic socialism, of socialism "with a human face," the last hope for the return of humanism to Marxism.

Before World War I, Dubček's father, a worker, an old socialist and later a Communist, sought his fortune in America like thousands of other Slovaks. He did not find it there. He had to work very hard, and the freedom and social justice of his dreams were not to be found. After World War I, he returned home to Slovakia and was one of the founders of the Slovak Communist Party. In 1925, like thousands of Czech and Slovak workers, he went to the Soviet Union to build the new society, taking along the whole family—his wife and two small boys, Julius and Alexander.

In the distant Central Asian territory of the Kirghiz SSR, Czechoslovak Communist émigrés founded Interhelpo, an agricultural and industrial cooperative. Many articles appeared in the Czechoslovak press about their pioneering work under arduous conditions and the enthusiasm with which they overcame difficulties. They were hailed as heroes whose internationalist ideals had been transformed into deeds.

The reality—less of which appeared in these enthusiastic reports—was slightly different. Some of the emigrés could not endure the harsh conditions and soon returned home. Only the most stubborn and enthusiastic endured, among them the Dubčeks. Then came the thirties and the Stalinist terror. In large measure it was directed against foreigners, who were regarded with suspicion by the agents of the NKVD because of their connections abroad. The Soviet secret police began to look far too closely at the Czechoslovak Communists in Interhelpo and to search for spies among them. Many from Interhelpo ended up in Soviet labor camps. The terror grew until the remaining Czechoslovak emigrés were faced with a choice: either to become Soviet citizens and sever all ties with their homeland, or to return to Czechoslovakia. The Dubčeks chose to return. They did not give up their Communist faith and were able to understand and forgive much, but they concluded that their place was at home.

The young Šanio (or Sascha, as his Russian comrades called him) had in the meantime completed his education in a Soviet school in the town of Gorki. He was sixteen when the family returned to Slovakia. Soon afterward World War II broke out. Alexander, together with his older brother Julius and their father, began illegal work in the Communist Party against the Nazis and the Slovak clerical fascists. In 1944 Slovakia rose against the Nazis. Both brothers were active partisans; Julius was killed and Alexander wounded.

After the Liberation, Alexander worked as a locksmith (a trade he had learned before 1944) in Slovakia and Moravia. In 1949 he became a paid functionary of the Party. He studied law at home. Then, because of his perfect knowledge of Russian, which had become his second language, the Party sent him to Moscow's Higher Party School, whose graduates are destined for the highest Party posts. After three years in Moscow, where he graduated first class, he returned home and was elected to the Central Committee of the Party in Slovakia. He subsequently filled Party posts and in 1963 was chosen First Secretary of the Slovak Party.

For a long time, Party functionaries had the impression that Dubček was growing up as a new man of the Antonín Novotný mold. But they were wrong. For in terms of building a career he lacked what Novotný had in unprecedented measure: personal arrogance, self-importance, an inner contempt for ordinary people and an *arriviste* hatred of men with wide intellectual horizons.

During the same years that these characteristics gained the upper hand in Novotný's personality and he became increasingly dictatorial, Dubček was developing in the opposite direction. Soon a priceless quality in a political leader was to appear, the ability to listen to diverse points of view. He had an inner modesty that permitted him to recognize the limits of his own abilities and his need to listen to the various opinions of the advisers whom a leader knows how to gather around him. Only after listening and exploring would Dubček reach a decision and carry it out. This characteristic, of course, had a dark side: precisely because Dubček listened carefully and at length, he gave an impression of indecisiveness and inconsistency. Before he reached a decision and acted upon it he seemed to succumb to different pressure groups.

For these reasons a new spirit grew up within the Slovak Party. Under the watchful eye of the Prague Central Committee, all the regulations of centralism, together with the less formal dictates of paternalism and authoritarianism, were faithfully followed. But even though in Slovakia as elsewhere Party functionaries supplanted the state and the administrative structure, even though the Party had become to a large extent apathetic, at least in Slovakia there were no great conflicts between intellectuals and *apparatchiks* and it was possible to breathe a little freely. One could hold a slightly different opinion without immediately being accused of deviationism and revisionism. Rehabilitated comrades could work more freely in Slovakia; it was easier for them and for the writers and scientists to see the First Secretary and air opposing views without being shouted down or persecuted.

So Alexander Dubček became the spokesman of wronged Slovak national sentiment and of the opposition to Novotný within the Party's Central Committee. To a characteristic ability to listen to contradictory ideas and viewpoints, and from them to make up his own mind, he added another quality that he obviously inherited from his Slovak peasant ancestors. Once his opinion was formed, even after long hesitation and vacillation, he advanced firmly and uncompromisingly toward his goal. Having chosen a course, he knew how to bang his fist on the table and how to walk straight to his destination. He was an unbending fighter.

The events of which Dubček became both the inaugurator and the victim only strengthened these qualities. On the one hand, they were the human substance of his tragedy. A man who all his life had been linked to the Soviet Union and the Communist movement now found himself ranged against both, as they were represented by official circles in Moscow. On the other hand, personal resolve strengthened his firmness, his stubbornness, his decision to continue along the path he recognized as correct and to follow it, if necessary, to a tragic end. Although Dubček still remained a staunch Communist with unlimited devotion to the ideas of Marx and Lenin, he began to interpret them in a manner that was abhorrent to Moscow bureaucrats.

Oldřich Černík's biography would not have betrayed that he too would become a leader of the Czechoslovak Spring. He grew up in Ostrava, where coal mines, iron smelting and foundries have driven out nature. He grew up in a working-class family and would have remained a worker had not the Communist revolution of February 1948 opened the way to higher education for the ablest children of the working class. Černík studied economics and, as a good Party member, the son of a Communist and a worker, took a job in the Party apparatus, working mainly in the sections that controlled industrial development. Černík proceeded along the usual upward path through the Party apparatus and became a member of the Ostrava regional committee. From there he came to Prague as a member of the Central Committee, eventually joining the Presidium, where he devoted himself mainly to economic questions.

Economics brought Černík into contact with members of the Academy of Science who were preparing the foundations of the new economic reforms. Like Dubček, Černík (a little unexpectedly to those who knew him) showed that he possessed the art of thinking undogmatically. He too could revise formulas, even those most deeply implanted, when confronted with economic realities and with other opinions. Moreover he demonstrated—to a greater extent than any other leader of the Communist Party of Czechoslovakia—political and statesmanlike insight. Realistically and soberly, he could judge given possibilities and calculate politically, without emotion or prejudice, evaluating all the circumstances. Only after mature consideration would Černík take political action, even if it agreed with his own fundamental persuasion regarding abstract principles. In the August 1968 crisis, Oldřich Černík proved to be the wisest Czechoslovak politician and the most realistic statesman.

The fourth leader of the Czechoslovak Spring, Josef Smrkovský, in contrast to his colleagues, was an old Communist of prewar vintage. He was a popular spokesman who could mobilize the masses even in the period when the Party was still in opposition or underground. Another feature of his life distinguished him from the others: Smrkovský went through Novotný's prisons, which steeled his character without changing his fundamental Communist persuasion. He, too, was of working class origin. As an apprentice baker of sixteen, he entered the Young Communist movement, took part in strikes, led demonstrations of unemployed youth, painted slogans, pasted up posters and fought the police. In the mid-1930s he became a professional Communist politician, first as secretary of the Prague Young Communists, later in other Party posts.

During the Nazi occupation, as the Gestapo liquidated leaders of the Communist Party one after another, Smrkovský remained in reserve. His turn came near the end of the war: in a perfect conspiracy, he escaped jail and became leader of the new, underground Central Committee.

The émigrés around Beneš in London and Gottwald in Moscow presented a united front during the war, even though there were differences between them. These were dealt with by negotiation and never rose to the surface or came into the public eye. The great powers did not therefore feel obliged to resolve these conflicts (as had been the case with the Poles and the

Yugoslavs). Obeying the joint appeal of Beneš and Gottwald, National Councils were formed as instrumentalities to carry on the struggle against the Nazis at home. At the end of the war, a Czech National Council was formed whose chairman was Professor Albert Pražák, a Beneš supporter, and whose vice-chairman was a Communist, Josef Smrkovský. This Czech National Council ordered the Prague uprising against the Nazis on May 5, 1945.

Despite strenuous effort, the local leadership was unable to contact London or Moscow for advice; it could not even reach Košice, in liberated territory, where the first Czechoslovak government since 1939 (formed in Moscow by agreement between the Communists and the politicians around Beneš) was already installed. The Prague uprising faced the superior forces of the Nazi Army which, under the command of Marshal Ferdinand Schörner, wanted to make Czech territory the last stronghold of Nazism. In spite of the uprising's initial success, the situation by May 7 and 8 was grave. It was not known which Allied units would relieve Prague. The Nazis meanwhile were threatening to raze the city, and the example of Warsaw suggested that they were capable of such an act.

At this point, the commander of the so-called "Vlasov Army," concentrated around Prague, came forward with a proposal to declare his forces neutral. General Vlasov was a captured Soviet officer who had allowed himself to be persuaded by the Nazis to organize anti-Soviet units composed of Soviet prisoners of war held in Germany. (As is well known, the Nazis treated Soviet prisoners with little regard for the Geneva Convention. Hundreds of thousands of prisoners died of hunger or disease; a number of them decided to betray their country.) The Vlasov units were used several times at the front, fighting side by side with SS detachments. Now, in the last days of the war, they were trying to save themselves in any way they could. Their offer of neutrality to the Czechs in May 1945 was one such attempt. Later, Vlasov's soldiers were captured by the Red Army, their leader tried and executed, and the men confined for many years in different Soviet camps.

In desperation (the citizens of Prague were fighting almost with their bare hands against overwhelming German forces), the leaders of the Czech National Council, isolated from the world and responsible for the uprising, decided to accept the Vlasov offer. At the same time, on May 8, they accepted the German command's offer of a cease-fire because they still had heard no news of the Soviet offensive that was to liberate the city on May 9. German units streamed out of Prague toward the west, where the Nazis hoped to surrender to the American Army.

The Red Army entered Prague and, two days later, Beneš' government returned home. The Czech National Council and in particular its Communist vice-chairman Smrkovský, found themselves in disfavor. The Russians blamed them for signing the agreements with the Vlasov Army and the Nazis. What followed was far-reaching. For some time there had been an agreement among the factions that the government of liberated Czechoslovakia would be composed of both those who fought at home and those who had been abroad. The eleventh-hour decisions of the Czech National Council had created a pretext that the Soviets readily seized. A government had, after all, been formed after very difficult negotiations in Moscow. It was composed of people who had spent the war in exile, and its reorganization would have demanded very complicated negotiations; also, the fact that the domestic resistance was suspect in Russian eyes played a very large part in subsequent events.

So Josef Smrkovský, like Pražák and other leaders of the Prague uprising, found himself outside the new government. He was made chairman of a department that looked after confiscated German property.

In 1950 Smrkovský was arrested. He spent three years in detention, constantly interrogated and tortured, yet refusing to confess betrayal or espionage. The officials who staged the investigation did not quite know what to do with him: he could not be grouped with the principal defendants in the Slánský trial because it was impossible to accuse him of Titoism, the chief charge against Slánský himself in the main trial. Eventually he was accused of sabotage, tried with some economic experts, and in 1954 condemned to life imprisonment.

Years later, on his release from prison, Smrkovský was still required to do manual work for a time, in spite of his age and ill health. In 1963 he was rehabilitated, even readmitted to the Party—thirteen years after his first arrest. During Lenárt's premiership, in 1966, he was made Minister of Forests and Waterways and elected to the Central Committee at the Thirteenth Party Congress. Some of Smrkovský's friends, especially former prisoners and rehabilitated Communists, reproached him for making his peace with Novotný and for beginning to collaborate with him. Smrkovský was of the opinion that he could more profoundly influence the regime by being inside the government, and in the Central Committee.

He did become in fact one of the main opposition spokesmen in the Central Committee. In contrast to men who had grown up, politically, under Stalinism, Smrkovský did not fear the vitality of the masses and could talk to the people. This old prewar Communist, a talented orator, became a popular speaker during the breakup of the Novotný regime and was soon elected Chairman of the National Assembly.

In the critical days of 1968, Smrkovský was the only top leader who had experienced imprisonment. That is why he returned from Moscow in August 1968 firmer than before. Smrkovský alone was not surprised by the way the Communist leaders of the Czechoslovak people were treated in the Communist prison into which they were thrown.

Chapter **9**

The Action Program

One of the first acts of the new leadership, after January, was to create within the Central Committee working groups charged with detailing the Action Program. The former leadership's policy mistakes had to be analyzed and a number of concrete measures proposed to overcome the economic crisis and prepare the ground for the Fourteenth Party Congress, tentatively scheduled for the middle of 1969.

The working groups were composed of scientists and social scientists. Their proposals were discussed in various committees, then worked out in detail by the appropriate departments of the Central Committee and, in their revised form, presented to the Presidium. They were approved at the Central Committee session early in April.

The Action Program became a kind of manifesto for the reforms that the new Party leadership intended to realize as quickly as possible. It became, too, a unique document in the international Communist movement. For the first time, concepts that Western Communist Parties had been debating for a long time were to be tested in practice. The synthesis of socialism and democracy sought by the Action Program could have become a blueprint for action programs of revolutionary movements in every industrial country with strong democratic traditions. Its ramifications could have extended (and the Czechoslovaks were not unaware that the eyes of the world were upon them) into positive reform in many societies. The tragedy of Czechoslovakia is partly one of missed opportunity, of a socialist experiment broken off abruptly whose results we shall never see.

The Program opened by stating the fact that, although antagonistic social classes no longer existed in Czechoslovakia (on the contrary, a rapprochement between social groups had begun), the formal organization of society remained unchanged from the era of sharp class struggle, from the early days of the dictatorship of the proletariat. Although the structure of society had changed, administration and direction remained static, bringing the whole society into acute crisis. The Party's perseverance in old methods and its use of political repression, centralized command and the limitation of freedoms had corrupted the authority of the Party's top echelon. Artificial tension had been provoked among social groups: between nations and nationals, between the generations and between Communists and non-members of the Party.

An all-embracing dogmatism had not permitted the country to abandon its unproductive theory of economic development. Orthodoxy held that the building of socialism depended exclusively on an accelerated, extensive development of the economy. This had caused a too rapid development of heavy industry that overtaxed the labor force, placed disproportionate demands on the supply of raw materials and made expensive investments of dubious economic value. However, the main reason that outmoded management existed in the economy was that the political system was also deformed.

According to the foreword to the Action Program, socialism can also evolve by creating latitude for people to fulfill their own interests. On this foundation, the country might forge the unity of all the working people by democratic methods. The goal of the Program was to create a new model of socialist democracy. This model would rely on the interacting work of experts and scientists, and of collective ruling bodies before whom the experts would lay alternative solutions to each important problem. The collective bodies would make decisions by democratic discussion. The task, said the Action Program, was to reform the political system in order to encourage the dynamic growth of social relations in a socialist society so that a broad democracy might be created, linked to scientific management by qualified experts. The new political system must guarantee that reversion to the old subjectivism and despotism would be impossible.

The Program spoke out clearly against the monopoly of power by one party or by a coalition of parties. If the Communist Party wanted to preserve its leading role, it was not enough to decree it, as Novotný had done, by writing it into the constitution. Nor could leadership be held by force; day after day, over and over, the Party must reassert its leadership by demonstrating its ability to mobilize the working class and to fight for its demands. True authority must be distinguished from control.

The National Front was an association of political parties that included, besides the Communists, the remnant of the old Catholic Party (called the People's Party), the Socialist Party, and other organizations such as the trade unions, the women's organization, the youth organization, etc. During Novotný's era the National Front was an empty formula by which other organizations blindly obeyed the orders of the Communist Party. Now the National Front was to be a live political organism with independent rights and independent responsibility for all its members. Under the new political model, the government must independently pass laws and control administration.

The new political model, said the Action Program, would safeguard the political rights of citizens. Freedom of speech took first place. The Program said it was necessary to end hidden politics carried on behind the backs of the people. All acts of government and Party organizations must be public, and citizens should be informed about official actions in detail. The Program severely condemned censorship. It proclaimed the freedom of scientific research and the right of every artist to create freely, thus presupposing open discussion and the right to err. Against the dictates of Party leadership, the Action Program proclaimed the individual's right to criticize even the most highly placed representatives of state and Party.

Legality must be renewed. Freedom of the press and of information could be limited by law only when it touched upon military and state secrets. The law was to restore the right of every citizen to travel abroad and to remain abroad according to his own inclinations. New norms for the rights of assembly were suggested. All those unjustly condemned in political trials were to be rehabilitated, and all who had suffered innocently were to be offered compensation. People who had participated in unlawful investigations and arbitrary imprisonments were to be prohibited from working in the judiciary or the police. The authority of the Ministry of Information, which in Novotný's time had been the chief instrument of political repression, was to be significantly limited.

From now on, the state security police would be concerned only with foreign espionage and was not to control the political acts and views of citizens. Prison staff, like the police, had hitherto been under the jurisdiction of the Ministry of the Interior; in effect, a man prosecuted in court was, even while serving his sentence, still in the hands of the people who had arrested and sentenced him. Now the penal system would fall under the jurisdiction of the Ministry of Justice. The independence of the courts was to be established and political pressure on judges to be made impossible.

A large section of the Program dealt with the rights of national groups, especially Slovakia. The Slovak nation was entitled to a national existence and autonomous rights, in accordance with previously proclaimed (yet unobserved) principles. The Action Program did not definitely advocate federation; a federal structure of the Republic was mentioned as an alternative to the tighter centralized structure of the common state. The Action Program also mentioned for the first time the need to guarantee national rights to minorities: Hungarians, Poles, Ukrainians and Germans.

The chapter on culture and education spoke of the autonomous rights of creative artists and of protecting them from the tyranny of bureaucratic interference. An education section urged that the whole education system be revised to meet the demands of the current scientific and technological revolution.

The chapter dealing with foreign policy proclaimed Czechoslovakia's resolute determination to remain within the group of socialist states; the Warsaw Pact alliance must be preserved, and economic cooperation increased within the Council for Mutual Economic Assistance (COMECON). It spoke of unity against imperialism, of the solidarity of the socialist states with national movements that were fighting for their liberation. Hostility to German militarism and revanchism was reaffirmed; on the other hand, Czechoslovakia proclaimed its active interest in general European security. It reserved the right to an independent Czechoslovak foreign policy that would be mindful of the interests of the whole socialist commonwealth and loyal to the Soviet Union. Yet, especially on European questions, Czechoslovak policy would consider the interests of the central European area.

A very long chapter of the Action Program was devoted to economic questions. In line with the economic reforms already accepted by the former Party leadership and by the Thirteenth Congress of the Party in 1966, the elements of both a planned and a market economy would be united. The state, by assistance and subsidy, would not help poor and uneconomic businesses at the expense of good and efficient ones.

For the first time in Czechoslovakia, the idea of workers' councils was mentioned. These would continue the postwar tradition of workers' committees, though council management would control and oversee the efficiency of each enterprise. The Action Program spoke too of a need to help weaker members of the working class. In the first place, lowering the standard of living was inadmissible. Pensions should be increased and workers should receive equal pay for equal work. The housing program would be accelerated, the social services developed, and so on.

The Action Program used language that was most unusual in a

country that had been governed for a considerable period by the Communist Party. Proclaiming the synthesis of socialism and democracy, the Program also attempted to find specific guarantees for it in law.

It was welcomed with very high hopes.

Chapter **10**

The Whole Society Is Shaken

All Czechs and Slovaks did not accept the announced changes with equal enthusiasm.

The greatest activity was manifested immediately after January 1968 among the intellectuals and young people, especially students. The intellectuals had suffered most under the arbitrary regime of Novotný; the Party leadership had mistrusted them a priori and demagogically agitated the workers against them. The leveling of earned incomes had lowered their social significance and importance. Scientific research was retarded by an officially sanctioned denigration of intellectual work and by bureaucratic planning of research priorities. Doctors groaned under floods of paper work; technicians were hindered by a stagnant economy; artists, writers and journalists were exhausted by struggling against a nonsensical censorship. Not surprisingly, among such people the promise of democratic freedom was enthusiastically received.

Young people reacted in the same way. They had suffered from excessive supervision that saw in initiative only the risk of departure from the beaten path. They had also suffered from the hypocrisy that hid inhuman acts behind socialist slogans. During the Novotný era, young people had turned away from political activity and indeed from all public life. Ostentatiously showing their distaste for the establishment, they opposed the official ideology by turning demonstratively toward religion and admiration of all things Western. Some young people, because of their opposition to the regime, supported the Americans in their war in Vietnam. When, in the spring of 1968, students demonstrated against the Vietnam War in front of the American Embassy, some North Vietnamese students pulled down the American flag and threw it into the Vltava River. Czechoslovak students scoured Prague for another flag and brought it (an old one with forty-eight stars instead of fifty), wrapped and tied, to the Embassy with apologies to the staff.

The young people felt the spirit of freedom for the first time. For the first time they heard speeches free of official hypocrisy; for the first time they offered their services and began to believe that society needed them. Something could be achieved after all by political work. The old official League of Czechoslovak Youth, through which Party bureaucrats had tried to gain youthful support for Novotný's Communism, disintegrated. New youth clubs sprang up and student activity increased. In the university halls there were daylong discussions of political and ideological problems.

Completely new organizations came into existence. Political prisoners freed by the amnesty or newly released united in K 231, an association that took its name from the number of the criminal code that dealt with treason. Some former Communist prisoners kept their distance from this association. The most prominent of them, Josef Smrkovský and the chairman of the Writers' Union, Eduard Goldstuecker, wrote critical letters to K 231. Although they recognized some justification for an association to oversee the civic and material rehabilitation of former prisoners, they still refused to join with people who had been condemned for anti-Communist activity or for cooperation with foreign intelligence services, even if many of these people had simply been victims of police provocation. Although K 231 clearly stated its aim as rehabilitation alone and publicly forsook any political stance, Communists continued to suspect that K 231 brought together anti-Communists who could use its platform for political gains.

Some tens of thousands became members of KAN, an association of politically committed non-Party members. The great majority of these were members of the non-Party intelligentsia, civil servants who had been overlooked under the former regime because they were not Party members. (One of the main principles of Novotný's policy had been that only Party members were to be entrusted with responsible posts in the state or economic administration.) Under the pretext that they represented the four-fifths of the nation who stood apart from the Communist Party, KAN demanded political representation. Representatives of KAN gave assurances that their aims were not opposed to socialism and that they recognized the political leadership of the Communists. They promised full support to Dubček's leadership, yet at the same time they spoke of the possibility of creating the political opposition that is indispensable to a democratic pluralist system.

Considerable political activity was shown by the two non-Communist parties of the National Front, the People's Party and the Socialist Party. They quickly discarded their former leaders, who had clearly been subservient to Antonín Novotný. In spite of the fact that these parties had been compromised by their role as puppets of the regime for the past twenty years, they now began to re-enlist former members who, after February 1948, had given up all political activity. People who until then had been considered second-class citizens now applied for membership in two parties. The People's Party rapidly gained members from the ranks of believing Catholics, especially in Moravia, and the Socialist Party drew upon the formerly self-employed. Yet the leadership of both parties expressed willingness to collaborate with the Communists then and in the future, within the rejuvenated National Front. The two parties welcomed the proclamation made by Dubček's leadership that the Communist Party would strive for the leading position in society, not by fiat or force, but in collaboration with other parties and organizations and in democratic competition with them.

The workers, however, remained apathetic and mistrustful somewhat longer. They followed the political developments with interest, yet they waited. The cause of their reluctance lay with the previous politicians.

In spite of the fact that the politicians had proclaimed the workers' leading position in society and appropriated for themselves the right to speak in the name of the workers, usually to flatter them, in reality they did their utmost to eliminate political activity by this important group. And the workers did not feel any better because the private factory owner had been replaced by a bureaucrat in a government office who only too often committed far more antisocial acts against them, in the name of socialism, than a capitalist would ever have dared. The trade union organizations, which should have defended the interests of the workers, had become so bureaucratic that in any labor dispute they defended the interests of the employers. Workers' meetings of the Party were limited to recitals of directives and distribution of administrative duties.

Toward the majority of people outside the Party, Communists played the role of wardens and commandants. The higher functionaries played the same role toward ordinary members of the Party. In such an atmosphere the workers were systematically encouraged to become apathetic, exclusively preoccupied with their private lives and the search for opportunities to earn more. The bureaucrats who held the top positions poisoned the whole working class with petty-bourgeois selfishness. The demagogy of the old Stalinists produced mistrust of new ideas in the workers. The Stalinists portrayed the events of January as the special concern of intellectuals and writers, who wanted to solve economic problems to the detriment of the workers and whose economic reform would lower living standards and create unemployment. After all, under the old methods of a directed economy, although the workers had to be satisfied with low wages, they were certain not to be dismissed for poor workmanship. They did not need to work to capacity, and they knew that bad morale and slack discipline were tolerated. All this suited some backward groups of the working class better than the uncertainty of an intensive economy.

Added to all this was the shock of the revelations of past mistakes and crimes. Day after day, Party and trade union functionaries and simple members of the Party were exposed to ceaseless bombardment by the press, radio and television. All the existing certainties, all the truths that had been drilled into everyone for twenty years, were suddenly in question. Leaders who as recently as yesterday had been thought infallible were now accused of having limited intelligence, of unbridled careerism, self-aggrandizement and crimes against humanity. Every day an unspoken, unformulated question was posed: Whose fault was it that prisoners were tortured? Who allowed the denial of the fundamental principles of humanism to hide behind the mask of humanistic teachings? If for twenty years it had been said that the Communist Party was the leading force in society, if nothing could have happened in Czechoslovakia except by decision of the Communist Party, was not the Party guilty of all that was now revealed?

This made a deep impression on the minds of numerous simple members of the Party and its functionaries. Some people gave up their Party membership after an especially dramatic television program about crimes committed in prisons and camps. If they remained in the Party, they said, they could not look their own children in the eye. After the January plenary session the Party press reported that the Central Committee was an example to the whole Party of how one should begin with self-criticism and move on to correct former faults. From top to bottom, the whole Party should follow the Central Committee's example, beginning by examining mistakes and shortcomings in its own practices. Yet the Central Committee's proceedings were hidden from ordinary members and nothing authoritative had been said about where blame lay. How were people on the lower rungs of the Party ladder to behave?

The communications media's exposé was sometimes made by suspect journalists with no Party allegiance. Party officials who for years had been accustomed to despise the opinions and views of anyone who was not part of the Party organizations now questioned whether these journalists had the right to interfere in the Party's internal affairs.

But the journalists were not the only ones who asked questions. Since 1948 about a quarter of a million former workers had climbed the social ladder; from standing by machines in factories they had gone to sit at desks in the state, Party, trade union, military and police apparatus. They had higher social status, better pay, lighter work, better housing and better opportunities for their children. These people taught themselves to work in a bureaucratic way, to give orders, to overlook public opinion, to listen only to orders from above and brutally to demand the fulfillment of their own orders.

Now the bureaucrats heard from above that their work had been wrong. They had brought the state and the Party into profound crisis and from now on would have to persuade and not order, to submit themselves to the democratic rules of the game. For twenty years they had been taught that they were the salt of the earth. Anyone who was not a Party member was *ipso facto* a second-class citizen who absolutely could not be trusted. Now they were told that a Party membership card did not entitle them to any privilege. The criterion for work was not membership any longer, but expert knowledge and the ability to act in a democratic manner. Could they unlearn old ways and follow the new ones? Could they learn to make decisions independently after years of avoiding responsibility by consulting an official in the Party apparatus over every minute detail? And if they could not adapt now, what would the future bring? The great majority of these people had lost their former skills. They were too old to return to factory work and too accustomed to a white-collar existence to adjust to a descent into the working class. It was hardly surprising that they became discontented, confused and apprehensive.

The police and judicial departments especially were affected by this feeling of uncertainty. The greatest criminals, men who had been responsible for the political trials of the fifties, were gone. But those who remained had been taught for years that they could behave almost lawlessly; their will was the law of the land against which appeal was almost impossible. Now, under the pressure of the revelations by the media, these people almost collapsed. Some committed suicide, fearing future exposure. Others, whose names were published, were working in well-paid jobs; they were boycotted by their colleagues and had to take leaves of absence. Some officers in the security apparatus were paralyzed by fear of the future.

And so the whole society approached a critical point. The unaccustomed flood of information carried daily by the communications media, the stormy political activity of the intellectuals and of youth had shaken everyone. The shape of things to come was being set in ignorance of the exact dimensions of the society that would emerge. Meanwhile the workers—the most important and numerous class of the socialist state—remained suspicious. They waited. The pillars of the establishment—the Party, the state apparatus, the police, security force and the mass organizations—were shaken by events. They had been the conveyor belt bearing the Central Committee's commands; now independent democratic initiative and action were expected of them. Transplanted to unfamiliar ground, they did not flourish and, to a certain degree, ceased functioning.

Under such conditions the greatest miracle of early Spring 1968 was the preservation of discipline. The masses had begun to move, and political involvement increased daily. On the other hand, the props of the old order had disappeared and its supporters were in disarray. In spite of the turbulent growth of ordinary people's activities, the daily exposure to revelations of crimes, the fact that idols were falling and the state apparatus was in crisis, public order was maintained. No stormy demonstrations took place, no one tried singlehandedly to settle old scores, no one was judged summarily, not one blow was struck.

With a remarkable sense of responsibility and discipline, Czechs and Slovaks argued in public. They read to exhaustion the newspapers that had suddenly become so interesting and sat by their radios and television sets late into the night. So deep-rooted were the democratic traditions of this people, so great was this nation's political responsibility and moral maturity that nowhere and at no time was public order disturbed.

Chapter **11**

The April Plenary

Confusion and disorientation were reflected by the Party's country-wide district and regional conferences in March. On the one hand the delegates protested that they had not been informed of what had happened at the plenary sessions of the Central Committee. It was unclear to them what crime Novotný had committed, and equally unclear was the Party's new course. On the other hand, Stalinist elements in the Party attempted to protest the amount of freedom permitted the communications media; they objected that the media spoke of matters that had long been taboo and interfered with Party affairs.

The main target of these attacks was the chairman of the Writers' Union, Professor Goldstuecker. In a television interview he had demanded the annulment of steps taken the previous year against the writers, and asked that the three writers expelled from the Party [Klíma, Liehm and Vaculík–Ed.] be reinstated. How dare Goldstuecker speak on television about purely domestic Party affairs, while millions of non-Party members were listening? A further reason for discontent among the old guard was the campaign against the police and security units and the revelations of their crimes. How dare the journalists defend people who had been condemned for treason, attacking Party members in the police and security forces who were only obeying Party orders? How was it possible to allow pilgrimages to the graves of Tomáš and Jan Masaryk? Was not socialism itself menaced by such permissiveness, did it not threaten the position of the Communist Party? The old guard, primarily functionaries who had learned under Novotný to rule without opposition, were fearful for their own future and for that reason tried to mobilize the Party against the reform movement.

But at these conferences a strong wing developed that comprehended this historical moment and understood that the Party now had a unique opportunity to regain the confidence of the widest possible mass of the people. It might possibly overcome the crisis in which it found itself through the faults of previous Party leadership. These delegates, mainly young people, demanded that the call of the Central Committee be answered and that democratic discussion occur at district and regional levels as well as at the top. Often at these March conferences young people stood up against the old functionaries who for years had suppressed any kind of protest or criticism. The old guard knew only how to dictate and command, and had almost changed the Party into a military organization where the main virtue was obedience, the main principle "Keep your mouth shut and serve." At some conferences words became acts; some old functionaries who had made profitable careers of their political function were dismissed immediately. Quite a few district and regional secretaries of the Party were not even elected to the new committees. For the first time in the history of the Party, the new functionaries were elected by secret ballot, which for years Novotný had stubbornly refused to allow.

At the beginning of April the Central Committee met in plenary session, in a completely different atmosphere from that of January. Then the whole country had passively awaited results that were not even fully disclosed. Now the country seethed. The communications media for the first time penetrated these sessions, the holy of holies to which previously only the initiated and invited dignitaries had had access. Now passionate public discussions took place anywhere and everyone waited impatiently to learn what the Central Committee would decide. Because the sessions were now public all speeches were to be published in the press, and radio and television would broadcast extracts from the sessions as well as interviews with individual members. Each speaker knew that millions of people listened to his words and compared them to his deeds. The end had come for politics behind closed doors.

The plenary session listened to the review given by Alexander Dubček. He asked for approval of the Action Program and spoke of the new political and economic model. He emphasized the necessity for a profound democratization of the whole society that would renew the great democratic traditions of the Czech and Slovak peoples. He spoke of the new role the Communist Party must play in order to regain the people's confidence. It must become once again the vanguard of the workers, so that it might again become the vital political organization it had been in the days when it was not in power or had shared power with other parties. He spoke of the Party's mission to return to "socialism with a human face," and of its humanitarian mission.

He even spoke of the fact that the Spring's opening of all the safety valves, and sudden freedom, presented the possibility that forces hostile to socialism might dream of turning back the clock to the pre-February 1948 era. Dubček explained that such recidivist hopes were encouraged by the fact that the former leaders' faults and crimes had compromised the idea of socialism in the eyes of all groups. Yet he warned against the crude suppression of these anti-socialist voices by force, because a box on the ears is not a political argument. Only by intensive work, only by a purposeful effort by all Communists would these voices be silenced in open discussion. He expressed his conviction that the strength of the socialist arguments would be effective and that the Communist Party would move to the offensive and regain for socialism those whom its distortions had repulsed.

The Action Program was unanimously adopted.

A few members of the Central Committee held out against the reforms, however. Of course no one dared to defend previous mistakes. Novotný himself, who took part in the discussion, had to acknowledge that mistakes had been made. But he too, like other members of the old guard, spoke against the "excesses" of the media, against the "campaign directed against the good Communists and faithful Party workers," against "the blackening and discrediting of the whole Party." He complained of "unnecessary fussiness" in the past, of the voices who dared to demand democratic pluralism or even an opposition, thus attacking the leading role of the Party. And so a conservative bloc was formed within the Central Committee by men frightened of further developments and afraid for their own positions, who hid their fears by pretended concern for the fortunes of socialism.

The April plenary session of the Central Committee altered the composition of the Presidium and decided changes in the government and in other state functions. The new composition of the whole organization was reflected in the fact that three strong, influential groups formed within the Party.

The first included those who fully realized that the new course must be carried through to the very end. They had in mind a new socialist model and the complete transformation of the Party into a democratic body able to lead the masses politically, yet at the same time able to apply internal democracy and give the minority the right to a different viewpoint. These people realized that they were inaugurating an experiment unheard of in the history of Communist parties: to give socialism back its attractiveness and its ability to influence the greatest number of people. The foremost representatives of this group were Čestmír Císař, Party Secretary in the city of Brno; Josef Špaček; and an old Communist who had fought in Spain, Doctor František Kriegel.

In the center stood the group around the First Secretary of the Party, Alexander Dubček. It did not have its own blueprint for change prepared, but it was willing to listen to opinions and then to reach a synthesis of different views. More than the first group, it was aware of all the internal and external dangers that menaced the Czechoslovak experiment.

The first group saw danger chiefly in the remnants of dogmatism and sectarianism, in the conservatism of the old Party workers who formed a majority in the organizations. For this reason they relied on youth and the intellectuals to purge the Party of the old conservatives and unimaginative bureaucrats.

Dubček's center group was more mediatory. It wanted to reach a compromise with the conservatives, being apprehensive itself and fearful of potential antisocialism. The people around Dubček were at that time still anxious about the popular stirring; they realized their inability to cope with activism in the society at large. They were still the prisoners of old dogmas, afraid that, if they were unable to manipulate the people (and they now knew that the disintegration of the Party apparatus had already progressed so far that they *were* unable to) the masses would move in unforeseeable directions.

Thirdly, there was a large bloc of conservatives in the Central Committee. In December and January these people had rebelled against the personal qualities of Antonín Novotný. After they had deposed him, they wanted to continue in the old ways. They were especially disquieted by the growing freedom of the press, whose revelations, from their point of view, were aimed at the very substance of socialism, or at least at the leading role of the Communist Party. Fundamental reform to them was foreign. In reforms they saw mainly a threat to their own privileged position, and they were mortally afraid of any new thought that opposed what they had been accustomed to for years. The sharpest criticism of the press came from this group, which most vociferously held that the internal affairs of the Party must not be spoken of publicly.

This neo-conservative group was represented chiefly by four men: Kolder, Indra, Švestka and Bilák. Drahomír Kolder was originally a miner from Ostrava, then a worker in the youth movement who had been made a Presidium member during the Novotný era. He devoted his time mainly to economic problems, yet he lacked an economic education and innate intelligence. Kolder played an important part in the struggle against Novotný, mostly because on a number of occasions he had been shouted at by the then First Secretary. He mobilized the Ostrava region, where he knew everyone who opposed Novotný.

Alois Indra grew up as a clerk in the Baťa shoe factory and in 1948 began a political career in the Party. He was a willing pupil of Bruno Köhler, a Sudeten German who was one of the worst Stalinists in Czechoslovakia. Even in the prewar years, Köhler had been a paid agent of the Soviet NKVD and, as such, after the war bore perhaps the greatest guilt for the political trials of the fifties. Until 1966 Köhler was one of the secretaries of the Central Committee; Indra served his political apprenticeship in Köhler's department. Later, Indra became secretary of a department of the Central Committee dealing with organization, the department that directed the entire Party machine.

Oldřich Švestka had been a clerk in the agricultural department of the Party, later becoming agricultural editor of *Rudé právo* and then, as a faithful servant of Novotný, its editor in chief. Švestka was famous for dogmatism. He was particularly guilty of persecuting journalists and writers who criticized the Party line, but he gained favor with Dubček because he once published an article on Slovakia that had angered Novotný.

Vasil Bilák came from eastern Slovakia on the frontier of the Soviet Ukraine, where there is a minority group that considers itself Ruthenian. Bilák himself belonged to this group. After World War II, under pressure from the Soviet Ukrainians, an attempt was made to persuade the Ruthenians to proclaim themselves Ukrainians. Most of these people were simple peasants who belonged to the Greek Catholic Church, as did the inhabitants of neighboring Galicia, which was annexed to the Soviet Ukraine. Because the Greek clergy in Galicia were bearers of Ukrainian national consciousness, an attempt had been made in Stalin's time to bring these Greek Catholics into the Russian Orthodox Church. The Greek Catholic Church has a liturgy similar to that of the Orthodox, but recognizes the Pope in Rome as its head. Stalin was angered by its allegiance to the Vatican and had the whole priesthood of the Greek Catholic Church arrested. He then forced priests of the Orthodox Church on the Galician peasants.

Because the Soviets had done this in neighboring Galicia, eastern Slovakia had to follow suit. At the beginning of the fifties, Vasil Bilák was given the task of "Ukrainizing"; himself a Ruthenian, he was then Party secretary for the Prešov district where the Greek Catholic Ruthenians lived. A good pupil of Stalin, Bilák carried out his job: Ukrainian schools were forced on the Ruthenians, although they had asked for Ruthenian or Slovak schools. The Greek Catholic priests who had participated actively in the resistance against Nazism were arrested and expelled to Bohemia, where they became foresters. Because Orthodox priests to force the new faith on the rebellious peasants were in short supply, Bilák sent state security agents and some Young Communists to a theological seminary, which he founded for this unusual apostolic purpose. After graduating from the seminary these people, in the robes of the Orthodox Church, were scattered among the villages to preach against the Vatican, praise the Patriarch of Moscow and the Communist Party, and help form collectives. It goes without saying that they met resistance from the peasants, who refused to attend the Orthodox services. Vasil Bilák then sent police and army units into the villages, forcibly to evangelize the rebellious peasantry with the new Word of God. Bilák's theological activity ended in bloodshed, mass arrests and forced collectivization.

This is the man who subsequently became ideological secretary in Slovakia. After Dubček's election at the January 1968 plenary, Bilák became First Secretary of the Slovakian Communist Party. Not only was he not a Slovak, only a year before he had expelled from the Party for bourgeois nationalism anyone who had dared to take a stand against Prague centralism and demand national rights for Slovaks. However, Bilák now sensed the wind of change and became the chief supporter of Slovak nationalism and chief spokesman for the idea of federation. It must be admitted that he was successful. While in the Czech lands democratic reforms were spoken of and minds were sharpened by democratic discussion, in Slovakia everyone—Communists and non-Communists, progressives and conservatives, Stalinists and anti-Stalinists—united in a national movement demanding federation. "First of all, federation; then we can think about democratic rights and reforms." Under this slogan Slovakia was united.

The situation had indeed changed a great deal. Before January Slovakia, with its national resistance to Novotný's chauvinism, was in the front rank of the opposition and helped to topple him. Now the same national demands put Slovakia in the conservative camp. In Slovakia the communications media spoke only of national rights; no associations were formed similar to KAN and K 231 in Bohemia and Moravia, and thus the apparatus of the Party and state was untouched.

These four people, who all in one way or another had taken part in Novotný's downfall, became spokesmen for the neo-conservative wing of the Party. At the Party conference in Ostrava in March, Indra and Kolder were the first to speak publicly against excessive freedom for the media. In Slovakia Bilák maintained the Party apparatus whole, undamaged and unchanged. Švestka, struggling with his staff, tried to make the chief Party newspaper a mouthpiece for those who warned against precipitate reforms. He, more than anyone, stood by the police and security forces; like Novotný, Švestka used demagogy in an attempt to persuade the workers that the economic reform proposed by the intellectuals was directed against the interests of the working class.

The compromises among the progressive group, the Dubček center group and the neo-conservative group were reflected in the composition of the new Presidium and the new government, following the vote at the April plenary of the Central Committee. All three groups were now represented in the highest institutions of the Party and of the state. The result, of course, was that this compromise carried differences and internal fights to higher levels of government. Consequently, effective government or rapid reform grew less and less likely. Instead of reforming and helping the Party, these factions deepened the crisis and weakened the Party's ability to lead and mobilize the people.

Chapter **12**

Thunder on the Horizon

After Alexander Dubček's election in January, leaders of the other socialist states felt it was time to meet the new Czechoslovakian First Secretary. In January Dubček went first to Moscow to be introduced to the Soviet leadership. He then arranged meetings with neighboring leaders: Kádár of Hungary, Gomułka of Poland and Ulbright of East Germany. Dubček apparently impressed his opposite numbers favorably at these meetings. The socialist leaders came to Prague for the celebration of the twentieth anniversary of the February Revolution of 1948, and they gathered again in Sofia for the meeting of the political leadership of the Warsaw Pact.

Until then everything went smoothly. The foreign allies even liked the fact that the deposed First Secretary, Novotný, had been retained as President, considering this a demonstration that nothing really important had changed in Czechoslovakia. But the country was in fact changing, and the lifting of censorship had loosed a flood of information and revelations. When, as a result, Novotný had to give up the presidency under pressure of public disapproval roused by the Šejna affair, Moscow, Warsaw and East Berlin became uneasy.

A conference was called suddenly in Dresden on March 26.

Representatives of five Warsaw Pact states* met for the first time to deliberate Czech problems. Rumania alone was not present, having been deliberately excluded because of its national and independent foreign policy. Representatives of Czechoslovakia were invited, and they faced a tribunal for the first time.

The details of the conference are not known. What is known is that the two fiercest guardians of dogmatism and orthodoxy, Walter Ulbricht and Władysław Gomułka, spoke aggressively against the Czechoslovaks. It is not difficult to imagine their attacks against the representatives of the Prague Spring, how they warned them against the dangers of freedom of the press and "revisionism." So far as Ulbricht and Gomułka were concerned, the Czechoslovak virus had begun to spread beyond the frontier of the Republic. Not long before, large student demonstrations had been held in Poland and meetings of writers had protested Polish censorship. The students' slogan, "All Poland awaits its Dubček," must still have rung in Gomułka's ears, in spite of the fact that the protest had been bloodily suppressed by police and mobilized detachments of the Party.

At Dresden the Russians are supposed to have been fairly mild in their approach, not pressing the attack too severely. But another surprise was in store for the Czechoslovak representatives. They were told by the Russians that Novotný two years before had agreed to allow armies of the Warsaw Pact to be permanently stationed on Czechoslovak soil. The Czechoslovak representatives, expressing their ignorance of this, said that according to the Czechoslovak constitution such decisions could be taken only by the National Assembly, and then only in the form of a formal international agreement. On their return to Prague, no document confirming the pledge was found in either the Ministry of Foreign Affairs or the Ministry of National Defense. Nevertheless, the Soviet representatives insisted that

---

* The "five states" of the Warsaw Pact, often referred to by the author, are those that ultimately invaded Czechoslovakia: the USSR, East Germany, Poland, Hungary and Bulgaria; Rumania and Czechoslovakia itself are not included. Ed.

the agreement stood, even if it had been only verbally given by the former President. The Russians would not be deterred by trivial matters, such as whether international agreements had or had not been signed. The Czechoslovak representatives were persuaded to agree to allow on Czechoslovak territory in June maneuvers of the Warsaw Pact armies—but the maneuvers were to include only army staffs, using a token number of foreign units. The confused Czechoslovaks acceded to this demand without realizing its future significance.

They had hardly returned to Prague when the first salvo against Czechoslovak "revisionism" was fired by Professor Kurt Hager, a member of the Politburo of the United Socialist Party of East Germany and one of Walter Ulbricht's closest colleagues. In a speech at an international gathering to commemorate the birthday of Karl Marx, Hager savagely attacked one of the prominent representatives of the renascence movement in Czechoslovakia, Josef Smrkovský, whom he accused of revisionism and excessive contacts with revanchists in West Germany. When Kurt Hager spoke he undoubtedly knew that Smrkovský had been chosen Chairman of the National Assembly, one of the most prominent positions in the state.

Hager's rude, Prussian attack was received in Prague by a storm of protest. Even Švestka's *Rudé právo* had to take a stand against Hager, and the Ministry of Foreign Affairs sent a note of protest to the government of the German Democratic Republic. Naturally, the East German press carried not a word of this protest. But the Czechs, now especially allergic to criticism from Berlin because of the thirtieth anniversary of the Munich *Diktat* of 1938, did not hide their anger.

Hardly a month later, pressure from Moscow began to increase. The four leading representatives, Dubček, Černík, Smrkovský and Bilák, were invited to meet the Soviet Presidium in Moscow on May 5. There they were presented with the exact timetable of the events of 1956 in Hungary, beginning with the February session of the Hungarian Central Committee at which Rákosi was overthrown, and ending in November with the Soviet intervention. By this analogy the Soviet representatives warned that events in Czechoslovakia were progressing at the same tempo; according to their calculations, the fiftieth anniversary of Czechoslovakian independence on October 28 would be used for a counterrevolutionary uprising whose aim would be to renew capitalism and to bring Czechoslovakia into NATO. The Soviets would be forced to intervene. In vain the Czechoslovaks, with the exception of Vasil Bilák, pointed out that the analogy was superficial. The Czechoslovakia of 1968 was not the Hungary of 1956; no counterrevolutionary menace existed in Czechoslovakia. Their sole aim was to cleanse socialism of the political degenerations and mistakes of the former leadership. The Czechoslovak leaders were sure that the Communist Party would retain its leading position. The Soviet representatives continued to shake their heads doubtfully.

Dubček and his companions had just returned to Prague when the first critical public barrage was fired, this time from the Soviet side.

The official speech of Čestmír Císař provided the occasion, at a solemn session of the Central Committee on May 6, the 150th anniversary of Karl Marx's birth. In this speech the ideological secretary of the Czech Party emphasized the great importance of Marx's teaching, which the Communists of Czechoslovakia were always to follow: "The period in which Marx lived and worked is over," said Císař, "[but] that fact does not in any way invalidate Marx's theory of society, his analytic critical methods. . . . The world of 1968 needs Marxism and realizes its importance more than any previous period." But he spoke, too, of twisted Marxism: "We cannot agree to everything that was done in the name of Marxism and for the victory of socialism. Not everything done has been beneficial to man and society. Not everything that pretended to be Marxism was true Marxism."

Then he spoke of Leninism as the creative interpretation of Marx's teaching during the era of imperialism. Leninism became the foundation of the victory of the Russian Revolution, and of the Soviet Union's great accomplishments. Yet "many Communist leaders were so blinded by Russian successes that they forgot the national peculiarities and different conditions in their own countries, and paid heed only to common and universally valid revolutionary principles." Therefore, in spite of the enormous importance of Leninism and in spite of its present validity, "one cannot deny some negative aspects of the fact that the experiences of the Soviet Communists were subsequently imposed as the only possible direction of Marxist thought and Marxist policy, and that Leninism had over the years been changed into a monopolistic interpretation of Marxism."

Císař went on to criticize the Stalinist revision of Marxism. "Every Marxist party must have its own policy, which takes into account national conditions and peculiarities and, of course, does not lose sight of ultimate revolutionary aims." Then he pointed out that the path sought by the Communist Party of Czechoslovakia must bring it closer to the Communist parties of the capitalist West. But at the same time he stressed ties with the Soviet Union: "If anyone in our country is speculating about the faults that have been committed, or attempts to belittle our alliances and our ties of friendship, then we shall reply that our Party takes these intentions as an attack on the chief guarantee of the state sovereignty and the socialist path of Czechoslovakia. Anti-Sovietism is, and will remain, the weapon of imperialism . . . close ties with the Soviet Union and with other Socialist countries are one of the cardinal conditions of the success of our revisionary process because they make imperialist intervention from outside impossible, and they give us the time and the security to carry our work to its final conclusion."

This speech was sufficient for the Soviet philosopher Konstantinov to accuse Císař, in a *Pravda* article, of revising Leninism. To Konstantinov, Císař's position represented servitude to world capitalism, enmity to world socialism and the Soviet Union. As a warning, he pointed to the precedent of what had happened to the German Social Democrats.

It was such an unbelievable statement, so obviously in contrast with what Soviet theorists themselves (Konstantinov included) had said only a few years earlier, that Party theorists in Prague were left breathless. A few days later in *Rudé právo,* Císař himself replied to the charges in a dignified, restrained essay. Prague philosophers in a letter to the daily paper *Mladá fronta* reminded readers that Konstantinov was renowned for revising his philosophical treatises to suit the momentary requirements of Soviet policy. After being an apologist for Josef Stalin, he reversed himself and offered philosophical arguments to back the fight against the "cult of personality." He had praised the theoretical depth of Khrushchev's speeches, only to turn about once again in order to excoriate the dangers of voluntarism—embodied in Khrushchev.

Almost simultaneously, the well-informed Paris paper *Le Monde* published a dispatch from its Moscow correspondent that reported a remark by General Aleksei Yepishev, commander of the political department of the Red Army. At an official function on May 7, the general remarked that if Czechoslovak comrades asked for help, the Red Army would come to their assistance.

This news item was, of course, denied by the Soviets. Ten days later, a delegation from the Soviet General Staff led by the Minister of Defense, Marshal Andrei Grechko, flew to Prague in order, they said, to meet General Martin Dzúr, the new Czech Minister of National Defense. A woman reporter for Czechoslovak Television asked General Yepishev at the airport whether he had made the statement reported in *Le Monde.* None too pleased, the general growled into the microphone that it was an absurdity. Obviously, for the first time in his life an ordinary journalist had stuck a microphone under his nose and asked him an impertinent question.

The moment the generals left, Soviet Prime Minister Aleksei Kosygin arrived. He had come, it was said, to take the waters in Karlovy Vary—he was even accompanied by his grandchild. Czechoslovak Television broadcast a Kosygin promenade through the spa in which the Soviet statesman spoke with a commentator about the weather, the quality of the medicinal waters, friendship

—and also about the responsible task of journalists. When Dubček and Černík visited him in Karlovy Vary (again, the public was told nothing about their discussions), Kosygin cut short his health cure and returned home. He said he did not wish his presence to influence the Central Committee session that was to meet toward the end of the month. Once again rumors arose that Kosygin had shown understanding of the specific nature of the Czechoslovak development, and that he had even promised that the Soviet Union would give Czechoslovakia the hard-currency loan so badly needed to overcome the technical obsolescence of the Czechoslovak economy.

In the meantime a delegation from the Czechoslovak parliament, led by its new chairman, Josef Smrkovský, departed for the Soviet Union. This visit had been scheduled for some time and was to reciprocate the visit of a delegation from the Supreme Soviet to Czechoslovakia in 1967. The delegation's tour of the Soviet Union was very carefully followed by the Czechoslovak press. To everyone's astonishment, the stories brought news of warnings given in speeches of welcome by Soviet dignitaries and of excuses and evasions in Smrkovský's replies. When the delegation returned, the journalists demanded that Smrkovský explain his assurances to Soviet representatives that the Communist Party of Czechoslovakia would fight against anti-socialist forces which, the Soviets said, endangered the socialist order; it was well known that these forces were insignificant and could not menace socialism. Smrkovský replied evasively and indicated that in the Soviet Union there were real fears for Czechoslovakia's future. The most radical newspapers in Czechoslovakia, *Literární listy* and *Student,* were ready to accuse Smrkovský of joining the conservatives by speaking in the vein of Kolder and Bilák. When Smrkovský visited the largest factory in Prague (the one where, some months before, Antonín Novotný had attempted a counterattack against the reforms) to give an account to the workers of his Soviet journey, he was shown to a small room where he spoke only to a group of chosen functionaries, not to the whole workers' collective. The next day Smrkovský complained to the press that he had been prevented from speaking to the workers.

On June 19 the Workers' Militia met in the hangar of Ruzyně Airport to hear the First Secretary of the Party, Alexander Dubček. The Workers' Militia was generally considered the most powerful support of the neo-conservatives. It had been formed in 1948 when the Communists were fighting for power, and was a kind of armed guard of the Party. Over the years its significance had grown less. The members of the Militia were, on the whole, men in their forties whose fighting strength was not great. Besides, the great majority were professional Party functionaries and administrative clerks in the factories: workers were in the minority. From the Workers' Militia came the most frequent attacks upon the media; the Militia threatened violence against anti-socialist forces.

Journalists were not admitted to the airport meeting. Alexander Dubček's speech was not published. Yet all over the Republic it was reported that at the meeting the commander of the Militia had joked that the Communists were divided into three categories: aquatic, those who float with the current; woodland, those who hide behind trees in order to take the Party by surprise; and granitic. Militia members belonged to the last category because they stood firm to guard socialism.

From the Ruzyně gathering a letter was sent to the Soviet Embassy. The Czechoslovak public heard of this only when the letter was published by Moscow's *Pravda*. The text assured the Soviet Union that the Workers' Militia would not permit anyone to spoil Czechoslovakia's friendship with the Soviet Union, nor to tamper with the achievements of socialism. The Czechoslovak public read the letter as a direct threat to all progressive groups, an attack by the conservative forces that were trying to block further advances of the democratizing process. Disquiet increased when, all over the Soviet Union, meetings were organized in factories in reply to the Workers' Militia letter. As reported in the Soviet press, these meetings of Soviet workers assured the Militia that their fellow workers would not permit counterrevolution to win in Czechoslovakia. They promised, if necessary, to help their Czechoslovak comrades. That sounded like a public threat of intervention.

In mid-June the "staff maneuvers" of the Warsaw Pact armies began. The commander of the Warsaw Pact forces, Marshal Ivan Yakubovsky, brought with him to Czechoslovakia numerous Soviet, Polish, East German and Hungarian generals. Reports in the Western press noted that foreign tanks had crossed into Czechoslovakia, too, in spite of assurances that only support and signal units would be called in. These reports were officially denied; a few days later, they were admitted. The auxiliary units grew to several thousand men.

When maneuvers ended on June 30 as planned, a press conference was called in Milovice, a military reservation near Prague, by the military command. Czechoslovak journalists were not admitted to Milovice, although Soviet and Polish reporters moved freely over the whole area. Czechoslovak officers answered the journalists' complaints by saying that they were not masters there and were powerless.

Then came the comedy of the armies' departure. The forces that were able to occupy the entire territory overnight needed a whole month to leave Czechoslovakia. Under various pretexts —repairs to engines and vehicles, or the excuse that the units could move only at night in order not to disrupt normal traffic —the foreign armies, like snails, crept east and west across the Republic and camped for weeks on end in the forests. To dismayed questions in the Czechoslovak press about a departure date for the foreign units, the Soviet press replied with malicious asides. The presence of Soviet armies was welcomed in 1945 and therefore their presence now could disquiet only counterrevolutionaries. Czechoslovak representatives of the government and the army, having often officially announced the withdrawal of the troops, were criticized by the public for not telling the truth. Yet this truth was refused them by their Soviet and Allied partners.

On August 3, the day of the signing of the Bratislava declaration, [see pp. 151ff. Ed.], the last Soviet units that took part in the maneuvers left Czechoslovak territory and bivouacked just over the Czechoslovak frontier. Storm clouds thickened above the Czechoslovak Spring.

Chapter **13**

Convocation of the Extraordinary Congress

The outcome of the April session of the Czechoslovakian Central Committee was a compromise between the different groups—the progressives, the hesitant center and the increasingly aggressive neo-conservatives. This compromise, as we have seen, was apparent in the composition of the new Presidium and the new government.

The whole opposition to Novotný had centered around the demand for the separation of Party and government. Now was the time to implement this demand and disperse power among many hands. Only two government officeholders, the Prime Minister and the Chairman of the National Assembly, would be allowed membership in the Presidium, the highest Party body, as well. And so it happened that only Oldřich Černík, as Premier, and Josef Smrkovský, as Chairman of the Assembly, were elected to the Presidium. In all other cases the attack against further concentration of power was successful. The academician Ota Šik, "the father of the economic reforms," who at the Thirteenth Congress had been the first to demand democratization of all public life and especially of the Party, now became Deputy Premier but did not become a member of the highest Party body which, after all, made the political decisions.

Before the April session, and even more after it, heated argument arose as to whether an Extraordinary Congress of the

Party should be convoked and whether there should be new elections for the National Assembly.

One consideration urged rapid convocation of the Congress: the actual composition of the Party apparatus, that is, the fact that the membership of the Central, district and regional committees (and equally, the composition of the whole apparatus of paid functionaries from top to bottom) did not guarantee that the Party would be able to renew itself quickly and thus become a driving force in the reform. The existing Party apparatus had been created in Novotný's reign; its composition and working methods were marked by Stalinism and dogmatism. One could hardly expect its people to lead society along new paths. This was exactly why the neo-conservatives opposed the convocation; they realized correctly that early convocation of an Extraordinary Congress would result in a depletion of their numbers, if not in their complete disappearance.

The Dubček center group was equally opposed to an early meeting. Its members did not yet have a clear perspective on how far they intended to take the reforms. Dubček clearly stated at the April session that the Party must not be hasty, that to prepare the Congress properly, to work out new statutes and new political directives time was needed. In consequence, at the April session Dubček had scheduled the Fourteenth Congress of the Party for the first half of 1969.

Nor would Dubček order any administrative change in the Party apparatus. He would not arbitrarily dismiss people (as Novotný had done) and he insisted on democratic procedures. He wanted to move slowly even if this entailed dragging conservative weight in the Central Committee and in the Party apparatus. In 1967 local government elections had been scheduled for May 1968 and parliamentary elections for autumn 1969. These elections were to be carried out by the old undemocratic methods, because only the old National Assembly could have changed the electoral procedures. Many conservatively inclined members sat in the Assembly and they could hardly be expected to pass a new, democratic electoral law.

Furthermore, the new regulations concerning the state and the federation of Czechs and Slovaks were a problem. It would be impossible now to elect a new Assembly according to the old centralistic constitution that denied national rights to the Slovaks. The elections were postponed until federation had been completed mainly because of Slovakian pressure for a speedy realization of federation.

Even after the April plenary session the progressives did not stop fighting for an advancement of the Congress in order to accelerate the rejuvenating process. The news media took up this demand, pointing out that there was no guarantee that the developments might not be put into reverse. People recalled 1956, when a rejuvenating process had begun in Czechoslovakia after the Twentieth Congress of the Soviet Communist Party. Then too discussion had raged within the Party, but the Party bureaucracy had succeeded in stifling everything and in turning the country back into the well-trod paths of dogmatism. Wouldn't all this be repeated? Four months after January 1968, it seemed that the only guarantee of a new direction was the sudden freedom of the press—yet even that was still only a verbal "gentlemen's agreement." In the statute books, the old press law and its minute subdivisions of censorship stood unchanged.

The progressive Communists saw the situation in Czechoslovakia this way: the process of democratization begun after January was so far-reaching, the activity of the masses so great, that sooner or later the question of who should have power must arise. Either the Communist Party would retain power for itself, creating a synthesis of socialism and democracy, or it would not be able to keep power, and the flow of events would then overwhelm it. New forces would arise, perhaps in an attempt to renew bourgeois democracy. The Communists would not voluntarily surrender power for domestic reasons, let alone international reasons, and they would be forced to suppress the movement by force, leading to the return of pre-January conditions —only, of course, even worse. Thus it was essential for the Communists to remain in power and try to create a new model of socialist democracy that would not imitate the parliamentary methods of the West, but create something new. However, the Communists would be successful only if they jettisoned the dead weight of compromised functionaries. They would also have to rejuvenate the whole Party and regain the confidence of the masses, legitimizing the Party's leading role in society by governing in a new manner.

By the same analysis the conservatives reached a different conclusion: that a precipitate convocation of the Congress must be opposed. In the first place, they knew that the Congress would remove their position and influence. In addition, they wanted to brake the process, not accelerate it. If they did not succeed in slowing it down then they must provoke a violent conflict and thereby restore a situation in which a bureaucratic police dictatorship held sway.

The real tug of war between the opposing forces, conservative and progressive, concentrated on this one question: Should an Extraordinary Congress of the Party be convoked, or not? The debate produced a public scandal.

A leader in *Rudé právo,* the central mouthpiece of the Party, demanded an early date for the Congress; the article appeared in the early edition and was read over the radio. Then editor in chief Švestka intervened and removed the leader from subsequent editions. The staff, supported by other journalists, protested this undemocratic intervention, viewing it as a return to censorship.

More and more even Dubček began to realize that, carrying such a large conservative bloc, the Party could not advance along the road proposed by the Central Committee. After all, Novotný and all his discredited colleagues still sat on the Central Committee. Yet they had been forced to abdicate their high positions in the Party, the government and the trade unions.

There was another reason for quick action. Revelations of the political trials and crimes of the secret police and judicial administration very seriously compromised the whole Party and shook its less sophisticated members. People constantly asked:

Who caused it all? Was Novotný personally responsible? After all, he had been at the helm of the Party for sixteen years and was its First Secretary at the time of the trials. Turning the pages of old reports of Central Committee sessions, they found in black and white that it was to Novotný's great credit and merit that "spies and traitors" had been unmasked. "Spies and traitors" had been official terminology for the innocent, as was now clear to everyone. Weren't the hands of Novotný and his helpers covered with innocent blood? If so, how could he remain a member of the supreme institution of the Party? While this question went unanswered, people's confidence in the Party was equivocal, and simple, honest functionaries could not be expected to work enthusiastically.

Yet against a too-hasty answer to the question of guilt stood the endeavor of the Dubček group to harm no one, not to hurry but thoroughly to reflect on everything. The question of where to place guilt for the 1950s demanded a close study of thousands upon thousands of documents in the archives. A special commission was appointed for this task: it announced that many months would be required to complete its work properly. Was the Party meanwhile to carry on its back this heavy burden of guilt? And if so, could one talk of a rapid renascence of confidence?

In these circumstances, an idea occurred to the Dubček group: bring pressure to bear upon the compromised conservative leaders to resign from the Central Committee and thus make it possible to separate the Party from the mistakes and crimes of its former leaders. Approximately twenty or at most thirty of the most compromised men would be affected. If they resigned voluntarily, the balance of power in the Central Committee would shift considerably and the neo-conservatives would lose their reservoir of has-beens. For precisely this reason, Novotný's men refused to render this service to the Party and its new leaders. Each one announced that he did not feel guilty; someone else was responsible, and as long as each of the former leaders was not convicted of individual participation in illegal acts, none intended to resign. Each said, "Why me, and not the others?" They hoped that, if collective guilt were assigned, each could escape individual responsibility and save his political career.

In this charged atmosphere Dr. Gustav Husák opened the Central Committee's plenary session at the end of May 1968. Husák, former Premier of the autonomous Slovak government and one of the leaders of the Slovak national uprising, was not a member of the Central Committee because he had become a Deputy Premier in the Černík government. He was preparing the proposals for federation. As a "bourgeois nationalist" Husák had been deprived of his office at the beginning of 1950 and imprisoned for more than ten years. Now he stood before the Central Committee to indict Novotný and prove his personal guilt for the trials and the executions. In his speech, Husák quoted letters he had written to Novotný from prison, giving evidence of his own and his fellow prisoners' innocence. The only reply to these letters had been a worsening of the prison routine. Even when, finally, the surviving victims of the political trials were granted amnesty and released, they continued to be persecuted by Novotný's regime.

After Husák's speech, the former President still had the insolence to rise and defend himself. Yet the situation was different now, and his phrases rang hollow. The Central Committee decided to deprive Novotný of his membership on it. Novotný and six of his colleagues, who were retired in any case, were also suspended from the Party until their personal guilt had been investigated. At last the Party had partly cleansed itself of guilt.

The surprise of the May session was that Alexander Dubček agreed to a hasty—if anything, too hasty—convocation of an Extraordinary Congress. The Congress was to begin September 9, which meant that all preparations had to be made during the summer months when most people were away on holiday. It was decided that the district conferences, which would elect delegates to the regional conferences, should convene in June.

The regional conferences, which would carry out the election of Congress delegates, were scheduled for the beginning of July. A special committee was elected to prepare the proposals for new Party statutes.

Once again the minutes of the Central Committee became a litany of the conservatives. They held that anti-socialist forces were gathering, that the very position of the Communist Party was menaced, that the Party was shaken by the revelations made by the media and that it was unnecessary to examine the past in order to focus on the future. Except for speeches delivered by some supporters of the progressive wing—who spoke of the new political model, of the need to secure civic, democratic rights, of economic reforms, of the need to transform the Party into a living, fighting political organism—the rest of the session echoed the nostalgic swan song of the old guard for the good old days when nasty journalists could not ask uncomfortable questions. It sounded, too, like a call to mobilization, summoning all members of the old order to the defense of socialism. In reality, the call was to defend all that these people imagined to be socialism: the old bureaucratic order of command, wherein the Party stood not among the people, but above them. The final resolution contained frequent warnings against the danger of anti-socialist forces.

A newspaper article calling upon factory workers to take the initiative and elect Workers' Councils provoked the anger of the First Secretary of the Slovak Party, Vasil Bilák. He accused the authors of undermining the leading role of the Party, of wanting to spread anarchy, and of helping anti-socialist forces. Of course he silently passed over the fact that the Workers' Councils were to be the cornerstone of socialist democracy. Yet no one protested this obvious demagogy.

Two published documents emerged from the proceedings: a proclamation containing the agreements reached at the sessions, and a resolution that dealt with the existing situation. Both bespoke determination to continue in the democratic process, to realize the Action Program and to pass at last from word to deed. Yet both documents spoke at the same time of a determination not to allow anyone to cast a shadow on the Party's character or to deny the Party the political and moral right to lead society. Should anti-Communist forces, said the resolution, "attempt an attack and want to lead the development of our nations in different directions, the Party will mobilize the forces of our people and of the socialist state and will repulse and suppress such an adventurist attempt." The resolution fundamentally rejected the effort to create opposition political organizations outside the framework of the National Front. The right to strike was recognized, but warning was given that strikes would damage the economy. Attempts to place workers and technocrats on opposite sides were pure demagogy. The resolution promised the legal abolition of censorship as soon as possible and appealed to workers in media to help the Party realize the Action Program instead of emphasizing negative aspects of the past. It stressed the duty of those journalists who were Party members to work actively against anti-socialist forces.

To what degree was this fear of an attack by anti-socialist forces justified? Was it only the conservatives' fear of the new?

The traditional May Day celebrations demonstrated the confidence of the people in the Party's new leadership. For the first time in many years these manifestations were truly spontaneous. Crowds surged along the main boulevards. No one was forced to take part; the people themselves chose to turn out. On a bright morning, a genuine public festival welcomed the new representatives of Party and state. The height of the reviewing stand occupied by the waving dignitaries was not Olympian, as formerly, and the street below it was thronged. People paraded, drifted off in casual groups, and close, friendly contact was made.

The very next day, several hundred students and young people staged a demonstration in the Old Town Square, at which anti-Communist and anti-Soviet speeches were made. Other anti-Communist attacks were heard at a meeting of former political prisoners. There were instances, mainly in the countryside, of angry citizens dismissing local Stalinists who in the past had been notorious for persecuting innocent people. In Slovakia there were isolated attempts to revive political Catholicism. But it was the attempts to resuscitate the Social Democratic party that made the new leadership most anxious.

The Social Democratic party had been united with the Communist Party after February 1948. In those stormy days the union came about in a not exactly democratic way: the left wing of the Social Democrats, aided by the Communist-led Workers' Militia, simply occupied the party headquarters and proclaimed unification with the Communists, forcibly throwing dissident Social Democrats out of their party. In the later years of Stalinism many former Social Democrats (even those who in 1948 had favored the liquidation of their party) were persecuted and imprisoned. Many were not permitted to follow their professions and thus became second-class citizens. In Spring 1968, understandably, these people saw the democratization process as an opportunity to renew their party. Some former Social Democrats issued a proclamation in which they rejected this aim and indicated the danger in it.

Doubtless an attempt to found a second workers' party would have been interpreted by Czechoslovakia's allies as an anti-Communist act and could have become a *casus belli*. Even some West European Social Democrats privately warned against such an adventure. Nonetheless, a group of former Social Democrats (mainly those who had spent long years in prison) stubbornly insisted on their right to revive the party and openly continued to prepare for the revival.

Over-all, the unmistakable preponderance of Communists and the clear decision of the working class to defend socialism (understood as common ownership of the means of production, with power to representatives of the working class) demonstrated unequivocally that the anti-Communist forces were a minute, neglected group. The more the Communist Party freed itself of past mistakes, the more profoundly would it be rejuvenated and the more quickly would it unseat compromised politicians. Extremes could be united by political means rather than by force. In a stable political situation and a normally functioning democratic system, such isolated forces would not endanger the existing system.

All, then, depended upon the leadership's capacity to regenerate the Party and to realize the principles of the Action Program quickly and thoroughly.

The leaders, however, hesitated and gave way to pressure from the left and the right alike. They were uncertain of the Party apparatus and of the anxious people in it. Irresolute, they shifted instead of containing the conservative forces that obstructed concrete reforms. Most of all the leaders feared the spontaneity of developments, and so became undermined by irresolution and compromise.

Chapter **14**

The "Two Thousand Words"

Many years before, the Party Presidium, under Novotný's direction, had decreed that all its members (and all members of the government) were duty-bound to speak on television and radio, at public meetings and press conferences. These proposals remained on paper and public appearances of the men in power were extremely rare—not surprisingly since politics was conducted behind people's backs and all official acts were veiled. Public men, when they absolutely had to, recited in bored tones the speeches written for them by their secretaries. If a politician improvised his speech and embarked on a talk "off the cuff," it was a near sensation that stirred people more than anything he might actually have said.

Now there was hardly a day when prominent Party members—ministers, secretaries of the Party and of mass organizations—did not make public speeches. For the first time the public learned something of the private lives of government men—their families, interests, hobbies, and how they spent their leisure. For the first time it was possible to publish unofficial photographs in which political figures appeared as ordinary people, not important statesmen. They were even caricatured in the press.

At the district Party conferences in mid-June, where delegates to the regional conferences were elected and delegates to the

Party Congress were recommended, unaccustomed political activity manifested itself. Delegates already were more outspoken than they had been at the March meetings. Discussion was often heated. In many places the conferences continued beyond their allotted time because such large numbers of people wanted a turn to speak. Everyone wished to express his views or come forward with his own proposals.

The Party had reached a critical point. Far more speakers now pronounced themselves against conservatism, outdated methods and the sectarianism of Novotný and his people. It was remarkable that now, in June 1968, even factory delegates supported the rejuvenating process, demanded the departure of discredited functionaries and the introduction of democratic working methods.

Still another phenomenon bore witness to the political ferment. Attempts to set workers against intellectuals were everywhere rebuffed. On the contrary, these equally important groups drew closer together. Many factories arranged socials and discussions to which they invited students, journalists, writers and artists for whom the Novotný leadership had made direct contact with the workers extremely difficult.

The secret ballot, formerly proscribed, now became the general rule. But in meetings and discussions people were understandably slow to learn democratic methods. Valuable time was lost in endless procedural discussion, and no one knew how to conduct democratic debate by means of rules of order. A kind of rudimentary democratic tolerance had to be shown to unfamiliar, opposing ideas.

A wave of spontaneous strikes was also a significant sign that the workers were abandoning the passivity with which they had, until now, regarded what was happening.

Of course strikes had also occurred when dogmatism reigned supreme. But then they were always wildcat and very brief. The Party and trade union functionaries rated them catastrophes, something that could not be tolerated. Strikes were broken by any means, rhetorical or violent. Regularly, at the end of a strike the state security police investigated to learn whether it had been organized by some domestic or foreign enemy. In more than one instance the leaders of such strikes were dismissed from their jobs.

Now, the right to strike was publicly proclaimed and the Action Program specifically laid down the duty of the trade unions to defend the material interests of workers. Organizations of the Party and the unions, like the state, lost their sense of security and were confused as to how they should operate. The strike leaders' fear of intervention and punishment from above disappeared. The widespread exhilaration of freedom had caught the workers at last.

In eastern Slovakia, workers in the East Slovak Ironworks went out on strike against the factory's group of Czech engineers and technicians, calling them anti-workers. In this case clearly nationalist, anti-Czech feelings played a part, as did the anarchistic mood of some workers, among whom were many gypsies and former farmers. In southern Bohemia, workers struck because under a new work program their product was to be manufactured in Ostrava. In Ostrava, miners went on strike against the director of their mine, whom they accused of incompetence. The director allegedly hid behind a talented non-Communist engineer who in fact managed the mine; and the miners chose that good and able engineer to be their new manager. In northern Bohemia, a strike occurred in a factory that produced valuable machines for export yet could not expand because, for bureaucratic reasons, it had been merged with a larger concern that restricted its production.

There were, of course, some strikes for higher wages, for better working conditions and similar issues that could not be settled favorably because of the insolvency of the particular enterprise and the generally torpid state of the Czechoslovak economy. The Party and trade unions tried to explain the damage caused by strikes: They greatly set back production, and, even when the workers' demands were justified, it was impossible to meet them immediately because the means to do so were lacking. Once again, the great discipline and maturity of the Czech and Slovak peoples manifested themselves; when the responsible officials and politicians mingled with the strikers to explain why it was not possible to fulfill their demands, the workers always accepted the argument and calmly returned to work to await a more suitable time. The strikes never provoked unrest or culminated in demonstrations and disturbances of public order.

These positive kinds of activity had a negative side as well. Some dogmatic Stalinists of the unalloyed variety began to write anonymous letters to prominent members of the reform movement. The letters were full of the coarsest anti-Semitism, threatening physical violence, a renewal of political trials and so forth. In January, immediately after the Central Committee's plenary session, such a letter (this time signed) was circulated by a group of five former Party officials, all now retired and drawing pensions. Their leader was a certain Jodas who before the war had been a clerk in the administrative department of a Communist newspaper. Jodas defended Novotný as the one true Communist and accused people like Professor Goldstuecker and Academician Šik of being counterrevolutionary. When this group had no success in circulating such letters among the different Party organizations, they began to write anonymous letters to individuals.

In June Professor Goldstuecker published in *Rudé právo* one such anonymous letter addressed to him, and condemned it as the work of people who had through dogmatic conservatism reached racism and Nazism. His article had a prolonged echo. *Rudé právo* and the other newspapers received thousands of letters expressing sympathy for the victims of these ugly attacks. Anti-Semitism, foreign to the traditions of the Czechoslovak people and to the spirit of Communism, seemed to be the curse of Cain on the followers of the deposed President.

In the middle of June a friendly meeting took place in Prague of professors and scientists, mainly naturalists, both Communist and non-Communist. As usual in those days, they discussed the political situation in the country. They were uneasy and discontented. The evolution toward democracy seemed to them too slow. Not one democratic law had yet been passed; at Central Committee sessions the majority of speakers avowed the need to restrain anti-socialist forces. The Workers' Militia, generally considered to be a bastion of conservatism, had just held a mass meeting to which journalists were not admitted. The Party leadership, in whom everyone had confidence, hesitated and retreated under conservative pressure. In the countryside and in the towns, old Stalinists still governed by the old methods. Anti-Semitic letters were increasing. Summer was approaching and with it a greater passivity. Rumors of a possible outside attempt to help the conservatives were widespread.

At this meeting of academicians and scientists someone suggested that the reformers appeal directly to the people in a proclamation that would stir them, warn them of the danger of a conservative comeback and call upon them to be more active in the fight for democratization. Scientists rarely write good proclamations. So they decided to turn for help to the writer Ludvík Vaculík, who had been the first sharp critic of the Novotný regime at the 1967 Writers' Congress. Vaculík agreed to help. He took about two weeks to write the proclamation, which was signed by its initiators and by other public figures. Thus the famous "Two Thousand Words" came about, the proclamation that played such an important role in later developments in Czechoslovakia.

The beginning of the proclamation criticized, in by no means novel terms, the situation into which society had been led by the Novotný regime. It called for greater activity: "We must go into the days to come with our own initiative and decisiveness."

The proclamation decisively distinguished its stance from the anti-Communist mood: "Above all we will oppose the opinion, if it should arise, that it is possible to achieve any kind of democratic revival without Communists, or even against them. It would be not only unjust, but also unwise. . . . The Communist Party of Czechoslovakia is preparing for a Congress that will elect a new Central Committee. Let us ask it to be better than the present one."

The proclamation opposed strikes, which could lead only to inflation. But it demanded elections of factory councils and the appointment of new, competent industrial managers. It insisted that the central Party and state bodies had done sufficiently important and progressive work; now it was necessary to allow them time to prepare new laws. It called also for an initiative from below, from the people themselves:

"If at this time it is not possible to expect more from the present central political institutions, it is necessary to achieve more in the regions and districts. We demand the departure of people who misused their power, damaged public property, acted dishonorably or cruelly. It is necessary to seek ways to induce them to go. For example: public criticism, resolutions, demonstrations, demonstrations by the working brigades, a collection for a retirement fund for them, a strike, a boycott of their doors. Forsake, however, all unlawful, insolent and rough methods. . . . Let us revive the activity of the National Front. Let us ask for a public session of the district committees. Let us set up special citizens' committees and commissions for the questions that nobody wants to recognize. . . . Let us support the security forces when they prosecute really punishable acts. We must endeavor not to create anarchy and a situation of universal uncertainty."

At the same time, the proclamation talked about the "great uneasiness of recent days arising from the possibility that foreign force would intervene in our development. Face to face with overwhelming numbers, we can only persist in our aims and not provoke. We can let it be known to our government that we will back it up—if necessary with arms—as long as it does what we give it a mandate to do, and we can reassure our allies that we will keep our alliances, friendship and trade treaties."

The proclamation was published on June 27, 1968 in *Literární listy* and some other Prague dailies. It would have passed without undue notice—as had a large number of similar articles—had not the neo-conservatives desperately been seeking a pretext to begin a campaign against anti-Communist forces that would speedily turn the clock back to the pre-January position. The "Two Thousand Words" became their pretext. To the conservatives, its call for initiative from below and for the removal of old Stalinists in the towns and country represented the greatest danger.

The National Assembly had met June 26, the day before the "Two Thousand Words" was published, and had finally changed the press law. Many members who had not shown overscrupulous concern for human justice in Novotný's time, and who themselves walked roughshod over the most fundamental human rights, now expressed a touching concern that the press might misuse its freedom to attack human rights. They demanded guarantees against libel. Of 244 members present, 30 voted against the abolition of censorship and 17 abstained. They were all Communists. The amended press law ended censorship and instructed the government to prepare proposals for a new press law.

The next day was to be the Assembly's closing session, followed by several weeks of vacation. That day the "Two Thousand Words" was published.

· After reading the article, a Slovak member of the National Assembly, General Samuel Kodaj, immediately requested a meeting of Communist members of the National Assembly. There he censured the proclamation as a counterrevolutionary attempt against the Party; he talked about anarchy, about a call to illegal action, and demanded the immediate reimposition of censorship, together with the arrest of all who had signed the proclamation. In addition, he asked the immediate convocation of the Central Committee and the postponement of the Extraordinary Congress. He found much sympathy at the Party meeting. Even Josef Smrkovský, chairman of the National Assembly and the leader of the progressive forces, in the first instance labeled the proclamation a "tragedy." The meeting of Communist members of the National Assembly, which lasted far into the night, issued an ultimatum requesting Party leaders to take a decisive stand against counterrevolution.

That same night Alois Indra, secretary of the Central Committee for Party affairs, sent a telegraphed circular to all district Party committees, warning them of the counterrevolutionary appeal. He gave instructions for extremely strong action against anyone who might try to collect signatures for the proclamation, and warned that delegates to the district conferences (which were to begin the following day) who signed the proclamation must not be allowed to attend.

On Friday, June 28, the Presidium issued a statement that condemned the proclamation as a call to counterrevolution. Irritably, the statement recalled the resolution of the May plenary session that decisive steps against anti-socialist forces would be taken. It appealed for the support of the Dubček leadership and mentioned the danger of anarchy and the disintegration of society.

On Saturday, June 29, there was a plenary meeting of the National Assembly, which refused to adjourn. A government announcement was made by the Premier, Oldřich Černík; in a calm, measured tone, it appealed for discipline. Be assured, it said, that the government itself knew how to guarantee order and to remove people who had not done their jobs. Černík's announcement quieted the hysterical atmosphere produced by the agitated announcement of the Presidium and by rumors that the Workers' Militia was mobilizing. (It was not.) The National Assembly then adjourned.

What happened next, however, was totally unexpected by the conservatives. The proclamation of the "Two Thousand Words," whose significance had been disproportionately magnified by the conservative outcry, rallied the workers above all others to its support. The radio news bulletin that the proclamation was considered an invitation to counterrevolution was enough to stir them: extraordinary powers to deal with the signers were asked by some conservatives and the conservatives wanted to put off the Extraordinary Congress. For the first time since January the factories protested—and protested against the conservatives. All day Friday and Saturday, all over the country, there were meetings of factory collectives, of Party and trade union committees in the factories. There people decided to add their signatures to the proclamation, to defend freedom of speech (a right now guaranteed by law), and to protest the ill-considered Presidium statement. Over the next few days, hundreds of thousands of signatures were collected. What was most important, the working class was now fully in the fight for rejuvenation.

The editors of the newspaper *Mladá fronta* received a resolution from a factory in northern Bohemia signed by the factory manager, the leader of the Workers' Militia and the chairman of the local Party committee. In the name of the whole factory the three demanded severe measures against the authors of the "Two Thousand Words." Next day, when *Mladá fronta* appeared in the town and the factory workers learned that someone had demanded reprisals in their name against the authors of the proclamation, they were so furious that they threatened to strike if the people who had signed the resolution did not leave the factory.

Why did the Presidium take such a position? Why did it brand as counterrevolutionary a pronouncement that appealed for support for the Party, that asked for observation of allied agreements—a proclamation written on the initiative of scientists and academicians who were loyal Party members?

The results of the unfortunate compromise between factions of the leadership manifested themselves here. The vacillations of men constantly subjected to various pressures and incapable of standing up to them were clearly revealed. Above all, the reaction showed a great fear of spontaneity and of any activity initiated by anyone outside the official leadership. Control of the Party might slip from the grasp of the Party leadership, which would then be forced to look helplessly to a mass movement for support. That is why the Party leadership preferred to give ground before this first decisive counterattack by the conservatives.

But soon it was clear that the workers had almost spontaneously associated themselves with the proclamation. At district conferences the representatives of the progressive trend were tremendously influential. Everywhere the conservatives were losing their position: 80 per cent of the newly elected delegates to the Extraordinary Congress belonged to the democratic wing. The outlook for the Congress seemed to seal the fate of the conservatives. Only then did members of Dubček's group in the Presidium realize their error in falling back under pressure from Indra and the others. Now there was no more talk of counterrevolution. On the contrary, some days later there was a friendly meeting between the writers and the members of the Presidium at which misunderstandings were clarified; it closed with the statement that both sides understood each other very well and shared the same goal.

However, the fateful Presidium announcement provided ammunition for the foreign allies, who were attentively watching all that was going on in Czechoslovakia. Dubček and his colleagues had given assurances at previous meetings that there was no threat of counterrevolution in Czechoslovakia, that the Party had the situation firmly under control and knew how to use ideological arguments.

Now the Presidium itself was talking counterrevolution. Instead of acting according to the May 28 resolution and mobilizing the workers against the anti-socialist forces (which, it was said, were grouped around the "Two Thousand Words"), they did nothing. In fact, the leadership ostentatiously fraternized with some members of the group. Did this not prove that the situation was out of the Party's hands? Was there not a danger of the Dubček leadership itself sliding into a counterrevolutionary position? No one in Moscow, Warsaw or East Berlin was anxious to read the "Two Thousand Words," no one in these capitals attempted to locate in the document itself the summons to a counterrevolution. The Presidium's ill-considered statement confirmed in their biased view those who sought proof of a counter-revolution: Czechoslovakia was set on a dangerous course.

After June, the existence of the "Two Thousand Words" played a significant part in the campaign against Czechoslovakia, a campaign that had been in preparation since May.

Chapter **15**

Change in Slovakia

The demand for changes in the constitution of the Republic, especially the creation of a federation of the Czech and Slovak nations, long remained an exclusively Slovak demand. Bohemia was indifferent to the idea. This was hardly surprising. For the Slovaks it was a question of national self-realization, the fulfillment of their national desires. For the Czechs, the question had arisen unexpectedly.

As a nation, the Czechs had achieved self-realization fifty years before, and the question of their national development had long been solved. During the first twenty years of the Republic, the Czech nation had been educated in the idea that there was no separate Slovak nation. Then came the war years and Slovak sovereignty: to simple people, Slovak national independence seemed to be the work of the fascists. Then, for the twenty years of the People's Democracy, they were told that the Slovak national question had been settled by the industrialization of Slovakia. Now they heard that industrialization solved the national problem only in part and that Slovak national aspirations went much further. A certain period of time passed before the Czech public understood that the creation of federation concerned it, too, and ceased to regard federation as a parochial interest.

The indifference of the Czechs had encouraged a growing

national consciousness in Slovakia that retarded the process of democratization. So Slovakia—which before January had been in the forefront of the progressive movement—found itself, after January, in the conservative camp. In Slovakia, nationalist propaganda obliterated all other distinctions.

Only when summer came did this situation change. The press brought the Czech nation to a knowledge of federalism. A Czech National Council was proposed, to be a partner to the Slovak National Council already in existence. While the Slovak Council had been founded as the result of general elections, the Czech Council could be created simply by the vote of the Czech members of the National Assembly; balloting took place at a special Assembly session on July 10. Dr. Čestmír Císař, ideological secretary of the Central Committee of the Czech Communist Party, was elected chairman of the Czech National Council. The conservative wing of the Party, while accepting the idea of a Czech National Council, refused to elect two important writers to the Council, Jiří Hanzelka and Pavel Kohout. The rejection of Hanzelka and Kohout, who were considered too progressive, caused a great public furore.

The problem of federation was complicated by the demand of some south Moravians who wanted a tripartite federation of three sovereign states: Bohemia, Moravia and Slovakia. This demand denied the national principle of dual federation because Czechs lived in both Moravia and Bohemia. It was rooted in the medieval division of the state. Under the monarchy, Moravia had been a separate margravate, with territorial and administrative autonomy that had been preserved intact until 1948.

Initiative for a triple federation came mainly from Brno, which, as Moravia's former capital, felt deprived of its traditional importance. But Moravia as a third partner in the federation was unacceptable to Slovakia. If Moravia were included, the national principle would be abandoned, and the Slovaks, in a triple federation, would once again find themselves outnumbered by their two Czech partners.

The Czech public took active steps toward constitutional changes and even began to speak favorably of federation, which helped the Slovaks to differentiate the federation issue from other important issues. Bratislava ceased to regard federation as the chief goal of the reform, which must be obtained, if need be in opposition to the Czechs, and for which Slovakian unity on every other issue had to be preserved. As good will between the nations grew, the democratization process was deepened.

The first person to understand this dynamic situation and to formulate it publicly was Dr. Gustav Husák. The most able and intelligent of all Slovak politicians, Husák had been imprisoned for a long time in Novotný's era, then barred from active politics. Now he was Deputy Premier in the government in Prague and entrusted with the preparatory work for the constitutional changes. Before January, Husák could only be in opposition, so far as the opposition had any room at all for maneuver. So he worked with the writers who were the advance guard of the rejuvenation movement and wrote articles in the writers' newspaper, *Kulturný život*. After January, writers who did not participate in actual politics wanted to continue the spirit of an opposition in order to be the progressive driving force behind the new leadership, and Husák and some of his friends took some political responsibility and demanded even more. For Husák to continue to identify himself exclusively with writers and the opposition would not have been responsible: indeed it was impossible for an ambitious politician with far-reaching plans. Instead Husák and his friends—to the great dismay of progressive public opinion, especially the writers'— dropped out of *Kulturný život* and founded their own weekly.

Now Husák, at the Bratislava conference, spoke incisively on the meaning and consequences of federation. Federation had been approved in principle; the final step was writing it into the constitution, which would be done on October 28, the fiftieth anniversary of the Republic. Because Slovakia was lagging behind the Czech lands in all other aspects of democratization, the time had come for fundamental changes in the Party apparatus in Slovakia. Husák proposed that the date of the

Slovak Party Congress be advanced so that it would be held before rather than after the Fourteenth Congress of the Czechoslovak Party, as originally intended. The purpose of this was to restructure the Party apparatus in Slovakia, to remove the conservative wing and to send to the Extraordinary Congress of the two parties a Slovak delegation composed of progressive supporters of democratization whose vision would not be limited by the national question.

Husák's proposal was not fully understood at first. Some Czech progressives detected a nationalist element in it. They felt he was dictating to the Congress about federalization: later events proved that Husák's Bratislava speech significantly influenced the removal of conservatives from the Bratislava Central Committee. The date of the Congress of the Slovak Party was fixed for August 26, before the Fourteenth Congress of all Czechoslovakia on September 9.

Another event accelerated the process of democratization throughout the state. On July 10 the proposals for new Party statutes were published; these were later to be presented for approval to the Fourteenth Congress. These blueprint proposals were to start a public debate of historical significance; for the first time in the history of world Communism, thoughts of a fundamental nature influencing the inner life of the Party and its position in society were openly formulated.

From the moment of their birth, Communist Parties had struggled with the problem of democracy, with the question of the rights of a minority to its own opinion as distinct from the opinion of the majority. In theory all Communist Parties recognize the right of a minority to its own position. This right, according to democratic centralism, is suspended once a disputed point is settled by a majority decision. Thereafter, not only is the minority not allowed to hold an opposing view, it is expected to fulfill in practice and to defend in public the majority opinion. Should the minority continue to propagate its different point of view, it becomes in a sense outlawed, outside the ranks of the Party.

Underlying the proposed new statutes of the Communist Party of Czechoslovakia was the assumption that truth emerges only from a confrontation of differing opinions. Thus, the new statutes would guarantee the minority not only the right to its own opinion before a decision was reached, but also the right to defend its opinion afterward. True, the proposals evaded the question of what methods the minority would be allowed to employ in defending its views. An answer to that question would have acknowledged the possibility of a different kind of organization and some type of genuine factional activity. Nevertheless, the very fact that toleration of minority opinion was proposed, together with the possibility of attempting to convince the majority of a minority view, signified a broad step along the road to real democracy within the Party. The right of the minority to an opinion sharply contrasted with Stalin's conception of Party discipline, which introduced a system of military command in a political party.

The proposals for the new statutes also changed the structure of the Party in regard to the preparations for federation and the separate existence of the Party in Slovakia and in the Czech lands. That was foreseen. The proposal spoke of two congresses for the two nations, of elections to two Central Committees, and of a federative congress that would elect the supreme organization of the whole Party, the federative Central Committee.

The new statutes proposed the principle of rotation of functions from high posts to low, and indicated measures to prevent an accumulation of power in the hands of one person. The relationship of the Party apparatus to the government was to be regulated according to the principles of the Action Program. The thrust of the proposals was to invigorate the Party as a fighting political organization that would lead by persuasion and political work, not by dictate. For the first time, too, the proposals admitted the possibility of resignation from the Party. Until then, voluntary departure had not existed; a Communist could leave the Party only by being thrown out of it.

By June it was clear that the Extraordinary Congress on

September 9 would indeed be extraordinary historically. Some 80 per cent of the elected delegates were progressive. The Congress would affirm the line inaugurated by the Communist Party of Czechoslovakia after January 1968 and approve new statutes that would democratize the Party. Hopes that the conservatives (at least in Slovakia) could hold their position had perished. The conservative forces who supported Stalinist dogmatism would definitely be excluded. The Congress, the supreme Party organization, would put its seal upon the development of democratic socialism. It would then be impossible to say that the intellectuals, the agents of imperialism or those seduced by imperialist diversions had infiltrated the Party, captured its leadership and turned the Party from the one true way.

If trends in Czechoslovakia ought to be reversed, if democratization should be stopped, if Czechoslovakia should be prevented from creating a new political model that would become an alternative to bureaucratic socialism, one that could be imitated elsewhere—the time had arrived to act. The Czechoslovak disease, the virus of freedom, must be prevented from spreading, at once. After the Congress would be too late.

Chapter 16

The Warsaw Ultimatum

Czechoslovakia was apprehensive in early July. Delays in the departure of the Warsaw Pact armies taking part in maneuvers continued, though the military exercises had ended June 30. Rumors spread that they did not intend to leave at all. In people's minds this was connected with the alleged verbal pledge of former First Secretary Novotný allowing troops to be permanently stationed on Czechoslovak territory. Was the Warsaw Pact a safeguard against external attack? Or was it an instrument to neutralize national sovereignty against the will of the constitutional leaders, and a means of controlling their armed forces and the stationing of foreign units on their territory?

Fears of the foreign units were augmented by the polemical tone used against Czechoslovakia in the press of the five allied states. Hardly a day passed without *Pravda* in Moscow, *Neues Deutschland* in Berlin, and *Trybuna Ludu* in Warsaw writing about counterrevolutionary activity in Czechoslovakia, proving, by quotations taken out of context, that the Czechoslovak papers were working to overthrow socialism. They were accused of insulting the Soviet Union and other socialist states. The "Two Thousand Words" incident was inflated beyond recognition. The authors of the article (whose unabridged text was naturally never printed in these foreign newspapers) were portrayed as men who called for an armed uprising against the government and demanded that the Communist Party of Czechoslovakia be disbanded and that Czechoslovakia become neutral. This hostile press campaign, together with the delayed departure of the armies and rumors of the concentration of additional Warsaw Pact armies along Czechoslovak frontiers, naturally heightened fears that something was being prepared against the rejuvenating process.

The Czechoslovak press tried to answer the journalistic polemics and to deny the false allegations. Czechoslovak journalists, writers, film and theater artists' unions invited their colleagues in Russia, East Germany and Poland to visit Czechoslovakia, see for themselves and then write the truth. Neither these invitations nor any retractions were ever published in the five states. The apogee of the smear campaign was reached in the press of the German Democratic Republic, which had opened it in March with Professor Hager's speech. Now the East Berlin press published sensational news: Czechoslovakia had opened its western frontier and an American armored brigade had crossed it. An invasion of Czechoslovakia by tank units of the West German Bundeswehr was in preparation, the East Berlin papers said. In vain Prague explained that an American film crew was in Czechoslovakia, shooting *The Bridge at Remagen.* The "American tank personnel" were actors in the film, along with Czechoslovak extras. The tanks were unarmed props and the whole enterprise represented an extremely advantageous financial proposition that would bring badly needed dollars into the Czechoslovakian treasury.

It was in this atmosphere that the Prchlík affair broke. General Prchlík directed the political section of the Czechoslovak Army and had resolutely opposed General Šejna's attempt at a military putsch to prevent Novotný's departure. After the January plenary session General Prchlík became the head of the Eighth Department of the Central Committee, replacing Mamula, who had been Novotný's right-hand man. Security and the armed forces came under the jurisdiction of Prchlík's section. The Action Program of the Party had referred to improper interference by the Party in the work of government and the National Assembly; a good example of this was the very existence of the Eighth Department, which in an authoritarian way directed the Army and security. The National Assembly did not even have a committee for the armed forces, such as exists in all other parliaments in which democratically elected civilians control the armed instrument of the state. Such a committee was not created by the National Assembly, and there was talk of abolishing the Eighth Department entirely.

In curious circumstances, this was accomplished. General Prchlík, now an ordinary member of the Party apparatus, was questioned at great length by Czechoslovak journalists about the departure of the foreign armies. Because he could answer the question, Prchlík revealed the fact that the Czechoslovak authorities had no influence over the Warsaw Pact armies. This admission, of course, acknowledged that Czechoslovak sovereignty was indeed impaired. The Soviets were furious. Their irritation increased when General Prchlík, at a press conference on July 15, said that the Warsaw Pact needed to be revised to strengthen the influence of civilian politicians over the military. (There had been talk of such revision for some time; the Rumanians especially advocated it. This was one reason that relations between Moscow and Bucharest had become increasingly cool.)

Soon thereafter, the Presidium of the Party announced that the Eighth Department had been abolished and that General Prchlík was being returned to his army duties. The abolition fulfilled the promise of the Action Program, but it assumed a different aspect in the light of General Prchlík's stand at his press conference. A very angry diplomatic note arrived from Moscow, accusing General Prchlík of betraying secrets of the Warsaw Pact and demanding that he be punished. There was talk that General Prchlík had demanded, in connection with the concentration of the allied armies along Czechoslovakia's frontiers, that the Czechoslovak Army be concentrated along its borders with Warsaw Pact states. Were this true, the abolition of the Eighth Department appeared not as an expected part of the

Action Program, but as a retreat of the Dubček leadership before unacceptable pressure from the allied states.

During the first two weeks of July, the five states of the Warsaw Pact prepared to discuss Czechoslovakia, which became the object of world-wide interest. In the West, one Communist Party after another proclaimed support for the Communist Party of Czechoslovakia. After visiting Moscow and Prague, Roger Waldeck-Rochet, the French Communist leader, proposed a conference of all European Communist Parties to evaluate the Czechoslovak situation. Presidents Tito of Yugoslavia and Ceaucescu of Rumania publicly stated their conviction that no counterrevolution menaced Czechoslovakia and expressed sympathy for the democratization that was going on; to them, it carried enormous significance for international Communism. The world grew increasingly apprehensive of a Soviet military intervention. The dilatory tactics employed by the foreign armies in leaving Czechoslovak territory seemed to be straws in the wind.

The Czechoslovak leaders, too, were invited to Warsaw. They refused, however, to participate in the meeting; once again, they foresaw that it would be a tribunal at which they would face prejudicial and insubstantial accusations. To excuse their refusal to attend, they cited their preoccupation with preparations for the Congress; also, they were convinced that they themselves were best qualified to judge the Czechoslovakian situation. With the help of the working class, they said, they could repulse any danger—from the left or right—and finally, they expressed willingness to take part in bilateral conferences on Czechoslovak soil. If a collective conference of all the socialist states was necessary, Yugoslavia and Rumania too must participate in it, and the prerequisite of such a conference must be reliable information; in this case, said the Czechs, none seemed available. It was imperative first to be well informed, and only then to judge.

This firm stand by the Czechoslovak Communist leadership immediately gained the people's sympathy. The world-wide excitement that Czechoslovakia had generated nurtured their patriotic enthusiasm. Thirty years before they had also been subjected to unsubstantiated accusations and unjust smears. The memory of the Munich *Diktat* and the subsequent capitulation were unusually vivid and relevant to them. Even convinced anti-Communists were now proud of the unyielding stand of the leaders of the Communist Party. One constantly heard ordinary Czechs and Slovaks say: "There is a difference between then and now. In a similar situation, Beneš capitulated: Dubček stands firm."

On Thursday, July 18, the Czechoslovak radio broadcast, in a special program, the letter of the five parties who had taken part in the Warsaw conference. Addressed to the Central Committee of the Czechoslovakian Communist Party, the letter was purposely not sent to the Presidium (which Warsaw knew had refused its invitation to attend the conference), but to the entire Central Committee. As everyone knew, there was still a very strong conservative bloc in the Central Committee.

The letter said reassuringly that, "We have not [interfered], nor do we intend to interfere in the purely internal affairs of your Party and your state, to violate the principles respecting independence and equality in the relations between Communist Parties and socialist countries." It was not that the five Parties wanted to prevent the correction of past faults and crimes, to suggest planning methods or the organization of the economy, or to prevent a settlement of the relationship between the two nations of Czechoslovakia. But the letter was concerned about earlier guarantees made by the Czechoslovak representatives at various conferences that they would "guard with their lives the Leninist principle of democratic centralism. Now, however, it seems, the Party is transformed into a discussion group."

The forces of reaction hoped to set Czechoslovakia against other socialist countries, the letter suggested. Political organizations and clubs outside the framework of the National Front had become headquarters of reactionary forces. Social democracy wanted to split the working class; anti-social, revisionist forces had captured the Czechoslovak press, radio and television and were systematically implementing a mortal terror among Communists. The "Two Thousand Words" was a political platform for counterrevolution, because it was an open appeal to fight the Communist Party, an invitation to strikes and disorders. "With it there arose a situation that was absolutely unacceptable for a socialist country," the letter continued. "How is it, comrades, that you do not see the danger? How is it possible to be passive in such a situation, to limit oneself to declarations alone, to assurances of loyalty to socialism and to allied treaties? How is it that you do not see that counterrevolution is capturing one position after another? That the Party is losing control over the development of events and is constantly in retreat under pressure from anti-Communist forces?" The letter closed with an ultimatum to the Communist Party of Czechoslovakia to mobilize against right-wing forces, to call a halt to the actions of all organizations opposed to socialism, to be master of the news media and to unite behind "the principles of democratic centralism."

The Warsaw letter unequivocally threatened to interfere with the internal affairs of Czechoslovakia—in direct contradiction to the resolution passed by the Twentieth Congress of the Soviet Communist Party, as well as to the 1956 declaration of the Soviet government. (The declarations of the world conferences of Communist Parties in 1957 and 1960 referred to the Parties' equality of rights, to the inadmissibility of interference, and to the sovereignty of socialist states.)

"We are convinced that a situation has arisen in Czechoslovakia that menaces the foundation of socialism and the interests of the other socialist countries. The nations of our countries would never forgive us indifference and frivolity, face to face with such danger. We are of the opinion that it is not only your duty but also ours, to resist decisively the anti-Communist forces and to fight equally decisively to uphold the socialist regime in Czechoslovakia."

The Czechoslovak Presidium's reply was published with the Warsaw allies' letter. It need not be emphasized that, although the letter from the five was widely publicized in those countries, Czechoslovakia's answer was either suppressed or angrily distorted.

The answer maintained that Czechoslovakia was passing through a contradictory political development caused by "the accumulation of contradictions in the years before the January plenary session of the Central Committee of the Communist Party of Czechoslovakia. . . . The broad movement of healthy socialist activity is accompanied by extreme tendencies to which remnants of the anti-socialist forces in our society are attempting to attach themselves parasitically, and at the same time dogmatic-sectarian forces linked with doubtful politics before the January plenary session are developing. The Communist Party of Czechoslovakia is aware of the danger and unanimously announces that it will fight against it. . . . We do not, however, see valid reasons to justify the assertion that our present situation is counterrevolutionary, the assertion of an immediate threat to the foundations of a socialist regime, or the assertion that in Czechoslovakia a change in the orientation of our socialist foreign policy is being prepared and that there is a concrete threat that our nation will be severed from the socialist commonwealth."

The Czechoslovakian answer rejected the charge that leading Czechoslovak circles were flirting with West German revanchists. It reminded the five that Czechoslovakia was the last country to establish economic contacts with the Federal Republic of Germany, "whereas other socialist countries had established them far earlier without arousing any fears." The reply again reiterated that Czechoslovakia would uphold all her allied agreements and, above all, would remain loyal to her alliance with the Soviet Union.

"We welcome the assurance," continued the answer, "that the five countries do not propose to interfere in the preparations for economic reform, or in the preparations for federalization." The authors of the answer attributed fears about the position of the Party in Czechoslovakia to insufficient information and understanding. "The Communist Party of Czechoslovakia depends on the voluntary support of the people; it does not fulfill its leading role by reigning over society, but rather by devoted service to its free, progressive socialist development. It cannot enforce its authority, but must unceasingly earn it by its deeds. It cannot lay down its Party line by commands but by the work of its members, the truth of its ideals"—this was a quotation from the Action Program. The reply continued: "Any hint whatsoever of a return to the old methods would evoke the resistance of the overwhelming majority of Party members, of factory and agricultural workers and of the intelligentsia. By taking such a step, the Party would menace its own leading political role and would evoke a situation that would truly result in a power conflict. In this way, the people's socialist achievements would really be threatened, and also our joint interests in the anti-imperialist front of the socialist commonwealth." The answer went on to describe in detail the Party's plan to carry out the Action Program, prepare the Congress, realize federation and resolve other problems.

As far as the "Two Thousand Words" was concerned, the reply reminded the accusers that the proclamation had been condemned by the Party: "It is necessary to realize that, after its rejection, no anarchistic acts took place in our country; and that the results of the appeal of the 'Two Thousand Words' did not menace the Party, the National Front and the socialist state."

As far as freedom of speech was concerned, the answer continued, extreme opinions had indeed emerged, and eventually a campaign against individual Party members, and "what could before be mentioned only as whispered propaganda, can now be publicly expressed." "If we ask the question whether it is right to evaluate such things as the ruin of the leading political role of the Communist Party of Czechoslovakia under the attack of the reactionary counterrevolutionary forces—we reach the conclusion that the answer is no. Because all this is only a part of our present political reality. There is, however, a second and—in our opinion—decisive part of the same reality: the growth of the authority of new, democratic party policies in the eyes of the broad mass of workers; the growth of the activity of the absolute majority of the population. The majority of our citizens from all classes and levels of society favors the abolition of censorship and freedom of speech. The Communist Party of Czechoslovakia is trying to show that it knows how to lead and to direct politics differently than by bureaucratic-police methods, by the strength of its Marxist-Leninist ideas, by its program, by its correct and widely supported policies."

The answer expressed regret that the Czechoslovak proposals for a bilateral meeting had not been accepted. There, all aspects of the Czechoslovak development could have been explained. The Communist Party of Czechoslovakia did not want to isolate itself from other parties; on the contrary, it wanted to strengthen the socialist commonwealth. The letter continued: "We consider that the joint affairs of socialism are not best served by a meeting at which the policy and action of any fraternal party may be judged in the absence of its representatives." It recalled that the Soviet government had declared in 1956 that all the Parties enjoyed equal rights; the Soviets would not intervene in internal affairs. The answer again reminded the allies that the 1956 declaration had been corroborated and solemnly announced at Party conferences in 1957. Again the Czechoslovaks proposed bilateral meetings at the earliest possible date.

The Czechoslovak government had passed a similar declaration in rebuttal to the Soviets; it refuted an accusation of deviant foreign policy and guaranteed that Czechoslovak foreign policy would not change. Similar declarations were issued by the National Front, the trade unions and youth organizations. On the evening of the same day [July 18], Alexander Dubček appeared on television to say that the masses had not previously been contented with the policy of the Party. Therefore "if the Party wants to carry out policy, it cannot change the masses, it cannot change people, it must change the methods of making policy." Dubček affirmed that the Party would continue along the path it had marked out in January. "The leadership of our Party, its democratically elected organizations, both the Party membership and the public and its representatives, are increasingly convinced that a real change for the better is taking place in Czechoslovakia; that socialism is discovering its true face, which is dear to everybody—that it is becoming stronger and sending out new, deep roots." Dubček called on all the people to support the policy of the Party leadership. "It would not help either our friendly relations or our future work to dramatize unnecessarily existing misunderstandings or short-sighted incitements of passions."

The letter of ultimatum of the five countries and Czechoslovakia's resolute reply revealed to the world the depth of the conflict between them. The dogmatic conception of socialism was pitted against an attempt "to give back to socialism its human face."

The Warsaw letter was purposely addressed to the whole Central Committee, not to the Presidium. The authors of the letter knew that the Presidium members on whom they could rely had not the courage to come out into the open. Their letter was addressed to the Central Committee chosen by Novotný, on which sat a sizable bloc of conservatives who knew that their role would end at the Congress.

The Central Committee, together with some Congress delegates elected at the regional conferences, met in Prague on Friday, July 19. The meeting aroused unusual public attention. The rooms at the Hradčany Castle where the meeting took place were besieged by thousands of people. Thousands of resolutions from district organizations, factories, the countryside, and tens of thousands of supporting letters from ordinary citizens reached the Party. The day before, the newly elected Central Committee of the Journalists' Union unanimously passed a resolution expressing support of the Party and pledged "not to divide forces in unnecessary domestic political wrangling, and not to give, at this time, any cause for polemics with allies."

Alexander Dubček spoke at the Central Committee session. He reassured those present, who were familiar with the exchange of letters, that the leadership hoped to settle the situation by sincere, open discussion. "Our Party always, consistently preserved the fundamentals of proletarian internationalism. During its entire existence it has never given any reason to be reproached for acts that would set it apart from the joint international working-class movement."

Dubček announced that, for Czechoslovakia, there was no road but alliance with the other socialist countries. But he insisted that the "indivisible ingredient of proletarian internationalism is the fundamental according to which every Party, while making decisions about its part in the building of socialism, must bear in mind the conditions in its own country. Socialism would be merely an empty abstraction if into it there did not enter the tradition, the historical experience and the spiritual atmosphere of a nation that is building a new, just socialist order."

He again emphasized that the Party was determined to continue in its policy. "A contrary step would mean that our people would really turn away from the Party and that we would be moving toward the discrediting of socialism in our country. And this would definitely not be an advantage to the cause of international Communism." He pointed out that the Communist Party of Czechoslovakia had never before enjoyed such universal popular support. He again repeated that the Party, conscious of the danger of anti-socialist forces, was wary of attempts to use dissension with the other Parties to provoke or to split the Party.

"We, members of the leadership of our Party," said Dubček in closing, "are daily made aware that we would not be able to stand at the head of our people had we not grown into one entity, were we not completely able to comprehend the wishes and longings of our people, and were we unable to link them with the interests of the international Communist movement. Just as in our own society, so in the whole socialist commonwealth, we do not consider it in any way abnormal that there are different approaches and opinions in individual questions. Therefore we do not see in discussion either a threat to unity or a disruption of the socialist commonwealth. Incorrect methods of settling different standpoints might lead to such tragic consequences—not, however, the different standpoints themselves. Historical experiences have today taught all of us in the socialist commonwealth that the results of such incorrect methods are deeply harmful both to each individual country and Party and to the whole socialist commonwealth."

Twenty-one speakers joined the discussion that followed. All unanimously supported the Presidium's point of view and its answer to the letter from the five—even leaders like Jiří Hendrych, formerly the closest collaborator of Antonín Novotný, and Drahomír Kolder, the main representative of the neo-conservative wing of the Presidium. (Because of his views, Kolder was not elected by his own Ostrava organization to represent it at the Congress.) In his announcement to the session of the Central Committee, Kolder stated that, although he considered the letter of the five true in some respects, the manner of the ultimatum forced him to support the viewpoint of the Party.

The final resolution, carried unanimously, approved the Presidium's reply and charged it with arranging bilateral meetings on Czechoslovak soil, at which time all misunderstandings could be resolved. The resolution again expressed a determination to hold fast to all agreements with the allies.

But the communications media of the five states who had sent the letter did not find it necessary to inform their public even now. The outside world applauded the firm stand taken by the Communist Party of Czechoslovakia; Yugoslavia and Rumania, as well as all the Communist Parties of the West, supported the position of the Party and sympathized with the Czechoslovak people. *Pravda* in Moscow reported the discovery of arms at Cheb in Czechoslovakia; these, it said, were being stockpiled by counterrevolutionaries preparing to oppose Dubček's leadership and Party. The news was confirmed by the Czechoslovak security force, too. But everyone in Czechoslovakia was convinced that it was a provocation intended to demonstrate the correctness of the letter of the five. After all, the arms had been found not far from the borders of the German Democratic Republic.

Chapter **17**

"We Are with You—Be with Us"

A unity came to Czechoslovakia that had never been known before. Perhaps there was not a single person who failed to comprehend the danger menacing the sovereignty of the state, the explosiveness of the situation. Dubček's oblique warning about "incorrect methods of resolving different points of view" was understood by all. Even the convinced anti-Communists realized that to take a stand against the Party now could endanger everything—even independence. The irresponsible attempts of the editors of the newspaper *Student* to publish—at this time—interviews with editors of Radio Free Europe (the American propaganda group, which often spoke against socialism in Czechoslovakia), stung all Czechoslovak journalists into a unanimous reaction. *Student* discontinued the articles. The Communist Party of Czechoslovakia had never, in all its fifty years, enjoyed such unanimous popular support. If free elections had been held in June, or early July, Dubček's people would have been elected to the National Assembly nearly unanimously.

Negotiations started for a bilateral meeting of Soviet and Czechoslovak representatives. Moscow insisted that all members of the Czechoslovak Presidium, without exception, must participate in the negotiations, though the Soviets themselves did not observe this condition. The purpose was obvious: to find, in direct confrontation, the weak spot, the less resolute member who could be won over and thus encourage a split in Czechoslovak ranks.

Moscow also insisted that the Czechoslovak leaders should come to Moscow or at least to some Soviet town near the Czechoslovak frontier. On this point Prague was immovable. There would be an upsurge of public opinion if the negotiators were to leave Czechoslovak soil, for it would be regarded as a sign of capitulation. Finally Moscow agreed that the negotiations should take place in Čierná nad Tisou.

Čierná had been an insignificant village in eastern Slovakia with some hundred inhabitants. Now it was a frontier post on the Košice–Uzhgorod railway line, the main marshaling yard for export and import trade between Czechoslovakia and the Soviet Union. Several thousand railway men and their families lived there, and a social center and houses had been built for them.

The confrontation of Soviets and Czechoslovaks took place on July 29. Once it was announced, tension again increased; everyone knew that all the reforms hung in the balance. *Literárni listy* published a special number containing an appeal to the Presidium: "We are with you, be with us." It was written by Pavel Kohout. Within hours, other newspapers reprinted this appeal; it was read on radio and television and a few students initiated a campaign to collect signatures to it. By Sunday night [July 28], when the entire Presidium left for Čierná nad Tisou, several hundred thousand citizens had signed the appeal.

"As has happened many times before in the history of mankind," said the appeal, "a few men will decide how millions of men will live. It is a difficult task and we wish to lessen your burden by our support. . . . The history of our land in the last few centuries is the history of freedom denied. Except for two short pauses, we were forced to create our national existence illegally. Many times we stood on the edge of the precipice. It is for these reasons that our nations welcomed so warmly the democracy that was brought us by the liberation in 1918. It was an incomplete democracy, because it did not bring its citizens political or social security. And yet it was, pre-eminently, the working class which in the days of Munich most concretely manifested their determination to defend the state against danger. And all the more eagerly did our nations salute socialism, though it did not give our citizens either civic or creative freedom. We stubbornly searched for it, however, and began to find it after this January. The moment arrived when our country, after centuries, became a cradle of hope again, and not for us alone. The moment arrived when we could prove to the world that socialism is the only real choice for all civilization.

"We expected that this reality would be sympathetically welcomed, especially by the whole socialist commonwealth. Instead, we are accused of treason. We have been receiving ultimatums from comrades who with every new pronouncement increasingly betray their ignorance of our development and situation. We are accused of crimes that we did not commit. We are credited with thoughts that we did not, and do not, have."

The appeal especially asked all Presidium members who were going to Čierná to convince the leading representatives of the Communist Party of the Soviet Union that "the rejuvenating process of the country must be taken to its conclusion because it is in our country's interest and in the interest of all progressive forces in all five continents.

"All we are striving for can be condensed into four words: Socialism. Alliance. Sovereignty. Freedom.

"In these ideas so vital to us lies our guarantee to fraternal countries and parties that we shall not permit a development that would menace the real interests of those nations in whose company, for over twenty years, we have been fighting for a common aim; and also the guarantee that there will be no repetition of the serious mistakes which only recently threatened to produce a crisis. . . . The extreme voices which here and there echo through our domestic discussions are the products of the bureaucratic system of policy making, which for so long stifled creative thought that it drove many people into opposition.

The authority of the Party and the position of socialism in our country is today infinitely stronger than ever before. We need democracy, peace and time, to become better socialists and more dignified allies than ever before. Speak in the name of the people who today have ceased to be an idea and have become, once again, the force that creates history. . . .

"Act, explain, but in unity and without retreating, defend the path on which we have set out, which while we live we shall not abandon. We are with you. Be with us."

Chapter **18**

Still They Negotiate

The meeting in Čierná nad Tisou began on Monday morning, July 29. The special trains of both delegations stood side by side, but toward evening each day the Soviet train left for the Soviet frontier station of Chop, to return the following day to Czechoslovak territory.

The first day of negotiations revealed how well prepared the Soviet side was, and the naïveté and inexperience of the Czechoslovak negotiators. The Soviet Politburo arrived with a large staff of experts and massive documentation, from which delegates read aloud throughout the first day, quoting from Czechoslovak newspapers, radio and television as though the articles and scripts were a brief for a prosecution. The Czechoslovak delegation was unprepared for this. They had hoped to convince their partners across the table by the force of their exposition, ideas and information. They had brought no formal documentation and could only deny the significance of the quotations from this accusing brief. The correctness or even the context of the quotes could not be verified.

Worse, when the Czechoslovak delegation tried to telephone Prague or Bratislava, or when the government in Prague and the Central Committee of the Party, in their turn, tried to contact their delegates in Čierná, they discovered a great deal of interference on the line. All over eastern Slovakia, between

Prague, Bratislava and Čierná, were numerous Soviet military units on the move whose communications equipment made direct telecommunication impossible. So the first day passed as a one-sided dialogue between two partners; one attacking and accusing, the other trying to defend itself—without success and without a great deal of conviction.

The second day was devoted to speeches by the leaders of both sides. About noon the First Secretary of the Soviet Communist Party, Leonid Brezhnev, fell ill. No one knows whether his indisposition was real or diplomatic. In either case, while he was present—but even more after his departure—some Soviet politicians sharply attacked their Czechoslovak comrades. Dr. František Kriegel, chairman of the Czechoslovak National Front and member of the Presidium, was their special target. Some of the Russians present did not hide their anti-Semitism, and in vulgar attacks upon Kriegel denied his right to speak at these sessions. This heavy atmosphere of personal attack was further aggravated when some of the Soviet negotiators struck at Alexander Dubček, accusing him of revisionism, of breaking his word, and finally of lying.

The Czechoslovak representatives were completely overcome. They had not imagined that negotiations between two sovereign states could be conducted in such a brutal and vulgar manner. Even the neo-conservatives in the Czechoslovak delegation were speechless. It may well be that, had the Soviets chosen different tactics, the Czechoslovaks would have been amenable to their arguments and might even have joined in condemning the Czechoslovak reforms. But in these circumstances they sat in silence.

So it went, until Dubček lost his patience. This man, so accessible to argument, so willing to listen to different opinions, had had enough. The conference had ceased to be a negotiation and had degenerated into a tavern brawl. Anger seized Dubček. He stood up, banged his fist on the table and said in Russian, *"Chvatit"*—"Enough"—and went out. The entire, stunned Czechoslovak delegation went with him.

Complete breakdown.

A little later, the chairman of the Soviet government, Aleksei Kosygin, came to the Czechoslovak train. He apologized for the personal attacks and insults—and argued that it was necessary to act in a comradely manner. A breakdown of talks might have unpredictable consequences. The Czechoslovak leaders agreed. Negotiations would be renewed in a completely different atmosphere.

At the same time, in Prague, members of the government met with the Party leaders who had stayed behind. There was no news from Čierná. Fantastic rumors were widespread, while the international news services reported continuous movement of the armies of the five Warsaw Pact nations along Czechoslovak frontiers. Attempts to reach Čierná by telephone had failed. Couriers dispatched by plane did not return. There was a real possibility of military intervention should the negotiations fail.

At this Prague meeting, it was proposed that a mobilization be ordered. The proposal was rejected, because of Prague's complete ignorance of what was happening in Čierná. Any mobilization could be interpreted as the provocation the other side awaited; and the Czechoslovak leaders all realized that the possibility of armed resistance—against manifold superior force and against invasion from almost every side—was infinitesimal. The meeting broke up on the understanding that, should it be necessary, a manifesto would be prepared containing a strong protest against intervention.

In the meantime, the negotiations in Čierná were renewed. President Svoboda spoke. He recalled the fraternity in arms between Soviet and Czechoslovak soldiers, the blood both had shed, the Czechoslovaks who died for the freedom of Czechoslovakia. Were these sacrifices to be vain? Would the love that had endured for centuries, the comradeship that Czechs and Slovaks felt for the Russian nation, perish?

With equal eloquence, General Svoboda proved the Soviet leaders' most important argument to be wrong. They claimed that Czechoslovakia had opened its frontiers with West Germany, and by so doing had seriously menaced the interests of the

Warsaw Pact states. General Svoboda stated that during the joint maneuvers in June he had inspected the Czechoslovak units on the frontier with Bavaria in the company of Marshal Yakubovsky, commanding officer of the armies of the Warsaw Pact. The marshal had admired the high morale and preparedness of the Czechoslovak units, Svoboda said. Who then was right: Marshal Yakubovsky or those who now said that the frontier was open?

Svoboda's speech brought tears even to some Soviet eyes. The tension was broken and matters were discussed in an atmosphere that contrasted sharply with the personal, vulgar attacks of the day before. The Soviet leaders advised watchfulness and sobriety, demanded firmness and resolve, and spoke against "decaying liberalism." The Czechoslovak representatives gave assurances that they would be guarded and firm and would not permit a counterrevolution of any kind. (Afterward, the Czechoslovak leaders assured the people that at Čierná they had not bound themselves to anything, that no document had been accepted—and that no notes, minutes or shorthand had been taken.) The Soviet side, predictably, interpreted the Čierná assurances as a commitment to proceed exactly as the Soviets wished. Both sides parted, each convinced that it had persuaded the other of the correctness of its viewpoint, from which neither wished to retreat.

The meeting adjourned on Thursday, August 1, and a further session was arranged for Saturday, August 3, in Bratislava, where other members of the Warsaw Pact—Poles, Germans, Hungarians and Bulgarians—would be present.

However, the Czechoslovak public, its nerves taut after four days of waiting to hear the results of the Čierná talks, knew nothing of the outcome. This news blackout arose from a difference in the position of the two negotiating parties. An open society had already been created in Czechoslovakia. Backstage politics had been condemned officially, and people now expected to be fully informed about events that would intimately affect their lives. But Soviet society remained closed: information released to the public was first assessed from all aspects, among which truth and complete disclosure were least important. So the communiqué issued from Čierná said absolutely nothing. Out of consideration for their partners, the Czechoslovak leaders could divulge little of the talks.

An unfortunate broadcast by President Svoboda on radio and television on Thursday evening, August 1, only made the people more anxious. The President spoke of the necessity of alliance and friendship with the Soviet Union. He called for discipline and prudence and thus gave listeners the impression that something had been decided at Čierná, something aimed directly against the national interests of the Republic. The whole Czechoslovak nation sank into deep gloom. People suspected that their leaders had agreed to something that *could* not be revealed and was therefore harmful to Czechoslovak interest. The most radical—the youth—compared the situation to the Munich betrayal of 1938.

The same evening, after the President's speech, thousands of people, mostly young, gathered in the Old Town Square. The speakers who addressed them, one after another, demanded that they be told the truth about the Čierná talks. Late that night an exhausted Smrkovský appeared on the balcony of the Party's city committee offices, which overlook the square. He pronounced a few optimistic phrases, which did not greatly reassure the crowd.

Later the same night, hundreds of young people gathered in front of the Central Committee building. This was nothing unusual; it had happened before in the open Spring of 1968— sometimes, when the Presidium met late into the night, a crowd of students would gather there. Sometimes Alexander Dubček or another leader had come out and talked with them, openly and honestly. But on this night none of these leaders was there. They were resting after four exhausting days in Čierná, but the crowd interpreted their absence as fear of the people, as an unwillingness to tell the truth. Slogans about betrayal were chanted and finally (it is said) some members of the crowd began to throw stones at the building. The police did not appear and the crowd dispersed. *Rudé právo* published news of the incident only after ten days, and the editor (Švestka) was careful not to say when the demonstration had taken place. So the Soviet press had further proof of counterrevolutionary preparations.

The atmosphere was not improved by a short interview with Alexander Dubček and Oldřich Černík, published the following day, or by Dubček's television speech on Friday, August 2. As neither man could fully report what had happened in Čierná, their speeches inevitably sounded false.

At this moment Moscow's *Pravda* published a letter from ninety-nine workers in the Pragovka factory in Prague to the Soviet Embassy. The letter denounced the Czechoslovakian enemies of socialism and of the Soviet Union. The letter appeared precisely as hundreds of thousands of Czechs and Slovaks were signing the appeal: "We are with you, be with us." Thousands of resolutions were pouring into the radio and television stations, demanding that the Czechoslovak leaders stand behind the slogan "Freedom. Sovereignty. Socialism. Friendship" in their dealings with the Soviets, and a spontaneous, voluntary collection, a gift to the Republic, was being taken—bringing in millions of crowns.

News of the *Pravda* letter echoed harshly around the country. In the atmosphere of patriotic enthusiasm, it sounded like treason, like willingness to collaborate. In the days after the Čierná and Bratislava discussions, a campaign was conducted against the people who had signed the letter in the Pragovka factory. The letter had apparently been written by two Party workers in the factory, old Stalinists who had persuaded some indifferent, apathetic colleagues to sign it. Several newspapers demanded that the authors be ostracized. In the factory, a meeting of all the workers excitedly demanded the dismissal of everyone who had signed the letter. The journalists present at the meeting sharply opposed this; they pointed out that tolerance of minority opinion is a fundamental of the democratic system. Because of the journalists' intervention, none of the signatories was punished. Only the two men who had written the letter, the commanding officer of the Workers' Militia and a Party secretary, were deposed. But the press of the five countries was able, once again, to write about the mortal terror to which honorable Communists in Czechoslovakia were subjected.

On Friday, August 2, delegates of six Warsaw Pact countries converged on Bratislava, where deliberations were due to begin the next day. The Czechoslovak delegation, flying in from Prague, was received by Bratislavans with a frenetic, affectionate demonstration. The delegates from the other five countries were far more moderately welcomed. Walter Ulbricht was received by the crowd in cold and contemptuous silence. Josef Smrkovský, in his role as official host, was thrown off balance by this icy silence. He turned to the members of the Workers' Militia who stood in silent ranks at the airport. "Couldn't you at least clap a little?" he asked. "No, we couldn't, Comrade Chairman," answered the Slovak workers, and smiled conspiratorially.

The Bratislava discussions lasted one day. In accordance with the Čierná agreement, Czechoslovak affairs were not on the agenda. The declaration accepted by the conference gave no hint of the special events in Czechoslovakia, but discussed in general terms the political fundamentals of the Warsaw Pact.

The deliberations, of course, were not easy. Both sides, Soviet and Czechoslovak, had arrived with prepared texts of possible declarations that differed in very many ways. The negotiations, therefore, involved lengthy debate as to the wording of individual items. What emerged was a document that could be signed by both sides, without either fundamentally departing from its original position.

For example, in dealing with relations with the Federal Republic of Germany, both sides agreed that it was necessary to fight German revanchism and militarism; both agreed to support the government of the German Democratic Republic. The Oder-Neisse frontier, Bonn's annulment of the Munich *Diktat* and the refusal of the Bonn government to recognize the German Democratic Republic were seen by both sides as threats to

European peace. But there was a sentence stating that even in the Federal Republic of Germany there were realistic, peace-loving forces that should be supported. Walter Ulbricht, indeed, agreed with this formulation, but insisted that the document unequivocally state who represented these realistic, peace-loving forces. He added that it was no secret that Czechoslovakia, Yugoslavia and Rumania believed the West German Social Democrats could be included among such forces. Ulbricht insisted that West German Social Democracy was led by traitors to socialism, servants of imperialism whose politics were as dangerous to European peace as the politics of the revanchists. In this attitude, Ulbricht clearly held the old position of the Stalinists. They had seen social democracy as the greatest enemy of the working class and devised the fatal epithet "socialfascist," which so encouraged the victory of Nazism by splitting the opposition to it.

The immediate result of Čierná and Bratislava was a lull in public polemics. World opinion regarded the result of the meetings as a victory for the Czechoslovaks. Czechoslovakia, it was thought, had been able to persuade her partners that her path was correct and that the nation was entitled to a unique, specific development suited to her conditions and traditions.

Chapter **19**

Ardor and Premonition

Now, at last, Marshall Tito's proposed visit to Czechoslovakia could be arranged. Several times the press had announced it, but each time it had been postponed.

Czechs and Slovaks had been traditionally friendly toward the Yugoslavs. Now this tie was strengthened and personified by President Tito, who had become a symbol of revolt against Stalinism. Tito himself, during the critical days of 1968, had already expressed sympathy with the Czechoslovak reforms. Tito had stated emphatically that the Czechoslovak Communists and the Czechoslovak working class could defend their socialist achievements alone. Unambiguously, he condemned any attempt at interference. The Yugoslav press, unlike the press of the five countries, wrote objectively and in detail of events in Czechoslovakia.

So Tito's visit, which took place some days after the Bratislava meeting, provided the occasion for a huge demonstration of defiance toward the dogmatism of the old, compromised methods and policies. Thousands of enthusiastic citizens of Prague welcomed Tito at Prague Airport and besieged the Castle where the Czechoslovak leaders and their Yugoslav guest were meeting. This guest, in contrast to some others, had captured the heart of the Czechoslovak people.

Their welcome for the Rumanian leader, Nicolae Ceaucescu,

was equally enthusiastic. He was not so well known as Tito. Nonetheless, Ceaucescu's independent foreign policy—which went much further than the Czechoslovak leaders had thought to go— and his open sympathy with the Communist Party of Czecho- slovakia in its attempts to revitalize the Communist movement made him too very popular with the Czechs and Slovaks.

In their public pronouncements neither statesman hid his sup- port for Czechoslovakia. They protested against interference and ultimatum and stood for sovereignty and the right of Czechoslovak Communists to decide, independently, what they should do for their own people. But in discussions with the Czechoslovak states- men neither guest hid his fears; each warned his hosts not to succumb to illusions and think that Čierná and Bratislava had resolved the conflict. They especially cautioned the Czechs not to think that they had come away victorious.

The feeling that all's well that ends well, that the conflict had been settled, was encouraged by the visit of Walter Ul- bricht. He had succeeded in inviting himself to a bilateral meeting with the Czechoslovaks, timed to fall between the Yugoslav and Rumanian leaders' visits. It did not take place in Prague, where the difference between the people's warm regard for Tito and Ceaucescu and their coolness toward the head of the German Democratic Republic would have been glaringly obvious. Instead, Ulbricht visited Karlovy Vary (formerly Karlsbad), the spa near the East German border. Ulbricht was the sole Communist states- man who had survived, unhindered, from Stalin's era into Brezhnev's.

Despite fears to the contrary, the meeting passed in an amiable, comradely atmosphere—as the official communiqué stated in its usual deadpan way. Unlike previous meetings (and unlike the tone of the East German press), Walter Ulbricht was polite- ness personified, interested in the Czechoslovak rejuvenating proc- ess, full of sympathy and friendliness toward the Czechoslovak comrades. He listened with understanding to information about the preparations for the Party Congress, eagerly heard an analysis of the new Party statutes, and assured his hosts that he was full of sympathy for their work. At the press conference he gave at the end of his visit, Ulbricht stated that the German Democratic Republic never used censorship—that dreadful institution. They had never had problems with their young people, who studied diligently and thought only about building socialism. In closing, Ulbricht told his hosts that at last he would be able to take a holiday because he was certain that the crisis was over and the misunderstanding resolved. Was this purposeful cunning to lull his hosts while the attack was being prepared? Or was he sincere, and did the chairman of the State Council of the German Democratic Republic himself not know that one week later he would send his army to invade the country to which another German politician had sent his troops?

The Czechoslovaks were understandably relieved to hear Ulbricht talk of a holiday—especially after news came from the Soviet Union that the chief men of the Politburo were taking their vacations, too. Yet when some members of the Presidium met journalists after Ceaucescu's departure, they were again in a pessimistic mood. The moratorium on polemics that had been agreed upon at Čierná did not last two weeks. The Soviet press took as its pretext for renewed attacks upon "revisionist" Czechoslovak journalists the incident of the letter to *Pravda* from ninety-nine men of the Pragovka factory. The Czechoslovak politicians begged the journalists not to reply to this new criticism. They received unanimous assurance that the journalists, aware of the gravity of the situation, would not aggravate it by polemics.

The politicians feared that provocation might be provided by some conservatives, at home and abroad, either to postpone the Congress or to divert the Congress' attention from the new statutes and the new policy. The journalists criticized the politicians for not fully exploiting the forceful support of the people at the time of Čierná. The leadership was criticized for not giving enough of the information the people were so anxious to have. Often, it was said, the leaders got lost in unimportant details and were unable to concentrate on vital matters. The politicians defended themselves by saying that they were more and more conscious of their mistakes but that they were only just learning how to govern by the new methods. They, like the rest of the nation, were attending the school of democracy.

To the direct question whether the danger of military intervention still existed, they replied with an equally direct and unambiguous NO. Intervention was out of the question, at least for the time being. This was on Saturday, August 17.

Chapter **20**

The Night of the Tanks

During the evening of Tuesday, August 20, the Presidium of the Central Committee was meeting in the Party building. Their agenda covered preparations for the Fourteenth, Extraordinary Congress and work reports from the people in charge of the main topics.

Alois Indra, secretary of the Central Committee, proposed at the opening of the meeting that, instead of discussing Congress preparations, the Presidium should study a document prepared by his section about counterrevolutionary attacks upon the Party. Indra's proposal was seconded by Drahomír Kolder of the Presidium.

A passionate debate followed. The neo-conservatives demanded that the document be discussed, while the progressive members of the Presidium rejected it as a deliberate diversion of their attention from the more important preparations for the Congress. The neo-conservatives accused Alexander Dubček of, among other things, seeking personal popularity by means of his liberalism. They claimed Dubček had used the issue to gain support among the intellectuals and non-Party members, and thus had sacrificed the interests of socialism. This was an obvious resumption of the personal attacks launched at Čierná.

Indra's proposal was finally voted down. The Presidium next turned to the First Secretary's report to the Congress.

After eleven o'clock, Černík left the room to make a telephone call. He returned almost immediately with news that armies of the Warsaw Pact had crossed Czechoslovakia's frontiers with Hungary, the Soviet Union, Poland and the German Democratic Republic. They were advancing deeper and deeper into the country. The civilian airport of Prague reported that two Soviet aircraft had appeared above the field and requested clearance for an emergency landing. Permission was granted, and as the planes taxied in, armed soldiers disembarked and quickly occupied the airport. A few minutes later, large military transport planes carrying crack units and tanks began to land.

The Presidium was stunned. With tears in his eyes, Alexander Dubček called this his personal tragedy, because his whole life had been linked to the Soviet Union. It was also a tragedy for Czechoslovakia and for the whole Communist movement, he said. The President of the Republic, Ludvík Svoboda, was reached by telephone and called to the meeting. After he arrived, it was decided not to oppose the occupation with arms. A proclamation to the people of the Republic would protest the occupation, and they would await further events in the Central Committee building.

At that moment a personal letter from Leonid Brezhnev was delivered to Alexander Dubček. In a tone reminiscent of the Čierná mood, the First Secretary of the Communist Party of Czechoslovakia was admonished for not keeping his personal word, pledged so many times, in Čierná and Bratislava among other places, to deal with the counterrevolution. But Brezhnev's letter contained not a word about the military intervention that was in full swing when the letter was delivered. Over half a million soldiers of the five states, armed to the teeth, and several thousand tanks had entered the Republic in order to implement the Warsaw ultimatum by force.

Late on Tuesday evening, August 20, as the Presidium had been ready to meet, the chief of the Czechoslovak Press Agency (ČTK), Miroslav Sulek, had suddenly entered the Press offices. Sulek was on a leave that had commenced when the Party organization of ČTK had expressed its lack of confidence in him—partly because of his Stalinist views, partly because of personal conflict between Sulek and his deputy who mutually accused each other of misappropriating official funds for personal advantage. The leave was to have continued until the affair was cleared up. Sulek spent his vacation in Russia as guest of the director of Tass, the Soviet news agency. His sudden return was even more surprising because he ordered that all news was to be brought to him for checking before release. When the ČTK editors refused to comply, there was a sharp exchange.

Shortly before midnight, Sulek produced a document and ordered ČTK to send it over the wires to the world. It was a proclamation of some unnamed "Czechoslovak statesmen and Party representatives," who appealed to the five Warsaw Pact states to send their armies to Czechoslovakia to suppress a threat of counterrevolution. The editors of the major dailies of the invading countries were eagerly awaiting this proclamation. *Neues Deutschland* in Berlin held its edition into the small hours of the morning. But the employees of the Czechoslovak Press Agency—the editors, translators and technical people—categorically refused to transmit the proclamation. Finally *Neues Deutschland* went to press without it.

After one o'clock in the morning, the Presidium finally agreed on the wording of an appeal to the Czechoslovak people. "It [the invasion] happened without the knowledge of the President of the Republic, the Chairman of the National Assembly, the Premier, and the First Secretary of the Central Committee of the Communist Party of Czechoslovakia and of other institutions of the state. The Presidium of the Central Committee of the Communist Party of Czechoslovakia considers this act in direct opposition not only to all the principles of relations between socialist states, but also as a negation of all fundamental norms of international law."

The appeal carried Svoboda's order to the armed forces not to offer armed resistance, and asked the inhabitants for calm and discipline. It announced the immediate recall of the National Assembly to active session, and of the Central Committee to plenary session. The appeal was carried, with four votes against it.

At approximately the same time the official Soviet news agency issued a statement: "Tass was authorized to state that the statesmen and Party representatives of the Czechoslovak Socialist Republic appealed to the Soviet Union and other allied states with the request for immediate assistance, including the armed forces, to the fraternal Czechoslovak people. This request is the result of the threat that arose because of counterrevolutionary forces who were plotting with foreign forces hostile to socialism. . . ."

The *Tass* statement did not name those "statesmen and Party representatives." Nor were they ever named. Later on, the conservative members of the Presidium, the conservative members of the Central Committee and of the National Assembly issued verbal and written statements, swearing on oath that not one of them had made such an appeal. Diplomatic notes announcing the intervention were handed to the governments of the Western nations by the Soviets that night. They too spoke of these "statesmen and Party representatives," but they were never named. After a few weeks even the pretense of their existence was dropped.

In spite of the fact that (according to the American press) President Johnson knew of the intended intervention in Czechoslovakia some hours before it began, the leader of the Italian Communist Party, Luigi Longo, who was in Moscow that day and met representatives of the Central Committee of the Soviet Party on Tuesday evening, learned about the invasion from his Wednesday morning papers.

At two o'clock in the early hours of August 21, the main Czechoslovak radio station in Prague announced that it was about to give important news from the session of the Party Presidium. The announcer read only a few words, and the station went dead. The cutoff was ordered by Karel Hofmann, the Minister of Communications, in whose study friends had gathered that evening to be told of the events to come. The Presidium proclamation was broadcast only by the local Prague radio station. At last in the morning the Czechoslovak radio, which was brought back on the air by technicians against the express wish of the Minister, broadcast the appeal to the nation.

In spite of the Presidium's joint decision to remain in the Central Committee building to await the occupiers' arrival, some members left. Among them were Premier Oldřich Černík, who went to his chambers; the editor in chief of *Rudé právo,* Oldřich Švestka, who returned to his editorial office; and Čestmír Císař, who went home to change his clothes and intended to return a little later.

Soon after Černík arrived at the building where the Premier's offices were located, it was beseiged by Soviet tanks. Soviet officers arrested the Premier, handcuffed him and took him in an army car to the airport, where they put him on an airplane that took off for an unknown destination. Švestka went to the *Rudé právo* offices to prevent publication of the Presidium proclamation, which he had opposed. In the building there was bitter argument between Švestka and the rest of the staff; it ended when Soviet soldiers transported the editor in chief to the Soviet Embassy, where Ambassador Chervonenko, handling the political side of the invasion, tried to put together a collaborationist government that included Švestka. In 1956 the Soviet government had sent a member of its Politburo to Budapest to supervise the whole operation. This time the Soviet government did not think that necessary; Ambassador Chervonenko would suffice.

After Švestka's departure, the rest of the staff used his absence to bring out a special edition of the Party's chief newspaper which contained the Presidium proclamation.

Shortly after his arrival at home, Čestmír Císař was arrested by two members of the Czechoslovak security force. News of this was broadcast in the early morning and everyone was certain that Císař was also among the kidnaped politicians. Later, it became clear that the Czech security men had taken him to a safe place.

Around four o'clock in the morning a Soviet Embassy car, accompanied by Soviet tanks, drew up in front of the Central Committee building. Soviet paratroopers rushed into the building. The First Secretary was on the telephone; it was snatched from his hand, and, in the best Hollywood gangster style, the paratroopers ordered everyone present to stand facing the wall and forbade them to talk. Automatic weapons in hand, soldiers guarded the arrested Czechoslovak leaders. After some time they were allowed to sit down and to order food.

In the morning Alexander Dubček, Josef Smrkovský and František Kriegel, wearing handcuffs, were taken by car to the airport and flown to an unknown destination. Just before he left, Josef Smrkovský (the only one of them who had been arrested in the fifties and imprisoned for many years) managed to put into his pocket three lumps of sugar, saying: "I know I shall need them." Other members of the Presidium and the staff were ordered to wait in the building. They were released Wednesday afternoon, August 21, and with the rest of the staff driven from the Central Committee building, which was then occupied by Soviet soldiers.

In the morning the badly shaken Czechoslovaks awakened to the thunder of tanks passing through the streets of their towns. Astonished at such treachery, full of memories of the Nazi occupation of 1939, huge crowds of people watched the army move in. Nobody fired a shot at the foreign troops. They, of course, fired many times, mainly in warning, especially when the crowd expressed its despair at what had happened. In those first hours, over seventy (according to some sources, as many as 120) unarmed civilians were killed. Hundreds of people were wounded.

In the morning, crowds gathered in Prague in front of the Czechoslovak radio, which uninterruptedly broadcast news about the occupation and the arrested politicians and appealed for calm. Before nine o'clock, Soviet tanks appeared not far away, on the sloping boulevards of Václavaské námĕsti (Wenceslas Square). Machine-gun bullets pock-marked the imposing façade of the National Museum fronting the square. In front of the Czechoslovak radio building, the crowd began to build barricades of trolley cars. Soviet tanks opened fire. Some tanks were gutted by bottles of gasoline thrown by demonstrators. Nearby buildings caught fire. After a short scuffle and some shooting, soldiers entered the radio building. The radio signed off by playing the national anthem.

To everyone's surprise, this radio silence lasted very briefly. Within hours, the Czechoslovak radio once again went on the air, to broadcast uninterruptedly for a whole week. But it broadcast now as the "legal, free radio." News, commentaries, interviews warning against eventual collaborators and appeals for resistance poured out. A miracle happened: for a whole week, under the noses of an occupying army, the radio survived. It became the main organ of resistance, the strongest cement of an unfamiliar national unity. For a whole week—constantly moving from one place to another, one district to another—announcers and commentators whose voices were universally known kept broadcasting. In exactly the same way, television continued to transmit for a whole week. The astounded viewer saw on his screen the faces of well-known announcers and commentators. Units of the occupation force searched diligently for these transmitters. Some they found and destroyed, but universal resistance made their task extremely difficult and finally impossible.

This unique episode in the history of communications was, ironically, made possible by the Communist Party's preparation —a plan made years before—of a clandestine resistance network that could operate in the event of an invasion by America and West Germany. Since 1948, a separate department had existed in every district and urban secretariat of the Communist Party, as well as in the local branches of the Association for Cooperation with the Army. This department maintained wireless transmitters, weapons, ciphers, codes, etc. against the day of a partisan war against Western imperialism. For twenty years a directive had ordered that this equipment be kept in working order, although the lessening of international tension in recent years had rendered it an illusory protection—and, in the event of a nuclear war, completely useless. But the directive had been strictly observed. When the plan was put into action, however, the invaders were not American but Soviet.

Czechoslovak army units also had a wireless network. With the help of the security forces and divisions of the Workers' Militia who protected the courageous journalists, radio and television technicians, it was possible to protect the transmitters. These groups transported them from place to place and warned of approaching danger. In this way, for a whole week, a powerful unifying and mobilizing instrument drew together the people in the struggle against the occupiers, and paralyzed all attempts by potential collaborators to work with the invaders.

The Czechoslovak press was not silenced either. In the large towns, the occupiers had seized the editorial offices and the printing presses. Nonetheless, the journalists were able to meet in private homes put at their disposal by the enthusiastic householders, or in the editorial offices of small specialized weeklies that were not occupied. One-page broadsides containing the most important news and information were printed on tiny presses. Soldiers, police and firemen acted as couriers between editorial offices and printers; eager volunteers offered to distribute the papers. There was not a day of the week when people did not get their newspapers. That first week of the occupation forged an unusual bond of comradeship, mutual respect and love between the journalists and other citizens.

In answer to an appeal by the news media, some general strikes of limited duration were declared. They appealed for the release of politicians who had been arrested and asked that the machinery of the state function again. Never before in Czechoslovakia's history had general strikes begun so spontaneously and unanimously as in those August days.

The terrible shock of occupation had a few unexpected and

positive results. An unprecedented sense of national unity developed, centered on the Communist Party, which placed itself in the forefront of the resistance. All classes and political differences —and the generation gap—disappeared. Communists and non-Communists, workers and intellectuals, the young and the elderly were united by their hatred of the occupiers. Young people, who had long been considered apolitical, interested only in sports or dancing or flirting with the Western way of life, were suddenly in the front ranks of patriots. Young people drove through the streets waving Czechoslovak flags; they brandished placards, debated with the occupying troops, distributed illegal newspapers, and helped to hide people who feared persecution.

The working class, which had also long been considered apathetic and suspicious, similarly stood up against the occupiers. Protest strikes in the factories were unanimous. The administrative machinery of government had broken down during the first hours of the occupation, so the workers had assumed the management of their industries and of transport in the towns. Wherever possible, they ensured a regular flow of supplies and continued production. The Workers' Militia, formerly the stronghold of Stalinism and conservatism, undertook to defend the Party secretariats and the clandestine transmitters. Due largely to their efforts, the Fourteenth Party Congress could after all be summoned and held—albeit secretly.

This occupation helped to erase national differences. The Nazi occupation of 1939 had exploited national differences and chauvinism and thus helped splinter the Republic. The 1968 occupation on the contrary drew together the nations who lived within Czechoslovakia. In Slovakia, interest in federation suddenly all but disappeared. The feeling of belonging to a single state was stronger than it had ever been among Slovaks, who stood (if that were possible) even more resolutely against the occupation than did Bohemians. During the spring and summer months, discord had arisen between Slovaks and Hugarians living in southern Slovakia. One would have thought that the occupation of the Hungarian districts of southern Slovakia by Hungarian troops would be welcomed, but the opposite happened. Suddenly the inhabitants forgot the differences that only yesterday had aroused nationalist frenzy, and the Hungarians stood as firmly as the Slovaks against the occupying divisions from Hungary.

The Czechs and Slovaks were perhaps the only nations of central Europe who had a centuries-old sympathy toward Russia. Russia had always been regarded as an older, stronger brother Slav. This bond had been markedly strengthened by World War II and the Nazi occupation. The Red Army's liberation of Czechoslovakia had transformed and fixed an ancient sympathy into sincere love and friendship. Now even sympathy had been destroyed. Profound shock and a sense of affection betrayed, which so strongly reminded the Czechoslovaks of thirty years before, turned friendship to raging hatred and contempt.

Chapter **21**

Political and Moral Bankruptcy: The Occupation

Naturally the intervention seriously damaged the Czechoslovak economy. The breakdown in transport caused perhaps the greatest harm. Air traffic was suspended by the occupiers, rail and auto traffic were greatly disturbed, and municipal transport stopped completely. In spite of all appeals that factory work be continued, the breakdown of transport and everyone's agitated frame of mind made this impossible. Besides the direct physical damage caused by the armies of occupation, the damage sustained by the Czechoslovak economy in the first week after occupation was estimated at two billion crowns.

On August 21 and 22, crowds of Czechoslovaks milled around the personnel of Soviet vehicles and tanks that stood in the city streets. They tried to convince the Russians that no counter-revolution existed in Czechoslovakia and that they had no business there. The Czechs' knowledge of Russian, which the Novotný regime had encouraged for twenty years, greatly helped them in these discussions, and they emerged the victors in debate. Most of the soldiers, Soviets and others, had absolutely no idea where they were or why (many thought they were on maneuvers, even that they had not crossed the frontiers of the Soviet Union). Some repeated the arguments their officers had taught them, which were extremely easy to refute. After the first few days, such discussions forced the Soviet command to rotate the occupying units with fresh reserves who had not yet succumbed to the "counterrevolutionary" arguments of an embittered people.

The Czechoslovaks switched from discussion and explanation to boycott. People ignored the occupying soldiers, refused to answer their questions, do them any service or sell them goods in the shops.

On the second day of the occupation, a rumor circulated that the occupiers, with the help of collaborationist groups in the Czechoslovak security force, were beginning to make widespread arrests. The radio quickly began a campaign to change street names and take down signposts. The rumor, however, proved false.

Very few collaborators existed in the Czechoslovak security force, largely because Minister Pavel some weeks before the occupation had succeeded in removing from the state security force about thirty of the most compromised officers. He had been prevented from doing so sooner by sabotage among the higher-ranking officials of the state security, and by the Presidium's lack of unanimity on the issue. Disagreement in the Presidium had been sufficient to bring about the appointment of a Slovak, Viliam Šalgovič, as Deputy Minister of the Interior for State Security. He was a Stalinist and a Soviet security agent. Šalgovič worked in direct opposition to his chief, Minister Pavel, but he did not succeed in winning over the security force to collaboration. On the third day of the occupation the government suspended him.

Under the slogan, "The postman will find it, let the rascal look for it," the young people on the third day of the occupation started a drive to change street names and remove house numbers and road signs. After a few hours not one road sign, street nameplate or house number remained in Prague. In their places appeared thousands of new plates that read "Dubček Street" or "Svoboda Road." In the country, all signposts were turned around, making it extremely difficult for the occupying forces to find their way.

Overnight, Prague and all the other towns—as well as highway asphalt, house walls, railway cars and engines, private autos and trucks—were painted with slogans or papered with handmade posters, frequently in Russian, protesting the occupation, glorifying the arrested national leaders, demanding the withdrawal of foreign troops and the renewal of sovereignty. Popular humor came into its own. The posters saying "Lenin, wake up, Brezhnev's gone off his head," "Ivan—go home," or the poster on the statue of Jungmann (the nineteenth-century spokesman of pan-Slavic thought), "Jungmann, Jungmann, you lived to see Slav solidarity," reflected the black humor of the nation.

In answer to the appeal by the Presidium, on the morning of August 21, a few dozen disoriented members of the Central Committee showed up at the Hotel Praha. (The Central Committee building had been occupied by Soviet troups who did not allow anyone to enter.) After some hours, a few conservative members of the Presidium arrived, escorted by Soviet officers. A discussion began. Some protested that they could not conduct business in the presence of foreign soldiers and demanded that the imprisoned Party leaders be released immediately. Others were willing to submit to the reality of occupation and to begin to collaborate. But the confusion was such, and the unanimous rejection of all collaboration by the Czech and Slovak working class so strong, that the meeting adjourned without a conclusive result. One member of the Central Committee remarked in closing that not only was the occupation real but also the people's resistance to it.

During the first night, August 20–21, Soviet Ambassador Chervonenko worked to form a collaborationist "government of workers and peasants" that would take power under the shadow of Soviet bayonets and put a seal of legality on the whole operation. Yet the potential collaborators, brought in Soviet cars to the Soviet Embassy by Soviet soldiers, did not show great enthusiasm for this scenario. Many were shaken. Patriotic feelings had arisen in them and their horror of betrayal proved too strong. Finally Chervonenko succeeded in drawing up on paper a future government led by the secretary of the Central Committee, Alois Indra. Many people were put on this list without their knowledge, and when they were told they angrily refused to join the "workers' and peasants'" government.

Finally, toward morning, Indra and Oldřich Pavlovský (Minister of Commerce and former Czechoslovak Ambassador to Moscow), went to the Castle to talk with Svoboda. They informed the President that Černík's government had resigned and that he was to nominate a new government with Indra as Premier. Svoboda, knowing that Černík had been arrested and kidnaped, said that he would accept Černík's resignation when Černík gave it to him personally. When Indra insisted on his own nomination, General Svoboda issued a brief command: "Out." Thus the attempt to create a semblance of legality for the intervention came to nothing. In the same way President Svoboda refused to negotiate with the Soviet Ambassador, to whom the traitors he had just thrown out of his office had returned, begging for help.

Early next morning, the National Assembly convened. Its chairman had been kidnaped but the members decided to act without him. From Wednesday, August 21, until Tuesday, August 27, when the government delegation returned from Moscow, the National Assembly sat in unbroken session. Members slept, ate, rested and worked in a building besieged by Soviet tanks. It was the same with the government: at times, up to twenty-two Ministers were meeting in the Castle. After the Premier's arrest, Madame Macháčová, Minister for Consumer Industry, took the chair.

Neither the occupiers nor the progressive Communists expected the next near miracle that occurred. There were many conservative politicians in the National Assembly and government who did not agree with the rejuvenating process and who knew that, after the Extraordinary Congress, their political careers would end. Yet they, too, rose against the occupation and at the decisive moment proved themselves patriots. Everyone had assumed that Zdeněk Fierlinger, formerly Premier and member of Novotný's Presidium for years, was one of Moscow's men in Prague. Now, as chairman of the Soviet-Czechoslovak Friendship League, Fierlinger went to the Soviet Embassy (where formerly he had been an almost daily guest) to protest the occupation. General Bohumír Lomský, Minister of National Defense in Novotný's era, had been replaced in April 1968. Lomský came to the National Assembly, of which he was a member; in full uniform, with all his Soviet orders on his chest, he delivered one of the most radical speeches against the occupation. When a Soviet major and some soldiers tried to disband the National Assembly session, Lomský shouted at him, demanding that the major stand to attention before him and obey his—a general's—orders. The confused Soviet officer retreated with his soldiers. General Kodaj had been the first man to call the "Two Thousand Words" a counterrevolutionary proclamation, and he had demanded the arrest of all who signed it. Now, as a district commander in Slovakia, he refused to deal with Soviet officers and gave his services unreservedly to the resistance. Bożena Macháčová, the only woman in Černík's government, had belonged to Novotný's circle and was universally considered an old Stalinist. She not only took over the premiership of the legal government in the absence of the arrested Premier, but personally read on the clandestine radio the government's sharp protest, which unambiguously labeled the occupation "an act of aggression against a state led by the Communist Party, executed by allied armies of socialist states."

There were many similar examples.

The President, the government, the National Assembly, the Presidium of the National Front—each protested the aggression. The anonymous "Party and state representatives" to whose invitation to enter Czechoslovakia the Soviet government had referred in its official announcement, in its notes to other governments and in its statements before the United Nations Security Council, remained anonymous. A puppet government had not been found. The whole people stood united against the occupation. The intervention was, from the political and moral view-point, completely bankrupt.

The convocation of the Fourteenth, Extraordinary Congress of the Communist Party of Czechoslovakia crowned and sym-bolized the resistance.

In spite of the fact that the Congress was to meet on Sep-tember 9, Party circles had often talked about convening it earlier. All the delegates had been correctly elected in late spring, and the Congress could thus become the highest author-ity of the Party at a crucial time. When foreign intervention disrupted the work of the Party Presidium and when consti-tutional bodies had to meet in semisecrecy, under siege, the Congress became in reality the state's highest representative body, even within the meaning of the official Moscow doctrine that defended the occupation as the answer to a threat to the Party's leading role. For that reason an early convocation of the Extraor-dinary Congress was justified. Because neither the paralyzed Central Committee nor the closeted Presidium was able to call it, the Party Committee of the City of Prague took the initiative.

The moment the "free and legal Czechoslovak radio" began broadcasting, it announced the decision of the Party Committee of the City of Prague to convoke the Congress for August 22. All delegates were asked to come to Prague, using any means of transport. The City Committee's building had just been occu-pied (on the afternoon of August 21). Delegates were told to come instead to the district secretariats in Prague. This appeal was changed periodically during the evening and night of August 21 as the Soviet army began occupying the district secretariats as well. Any of the bigger Prague factories was now receiving the delegates.

And so, on Thursday, August 22, at 11 o'clock in the morning, the Fourteenth, Extraordinary Congress opened in a factory in the Vysočany district of Prague—the same factory where Novotný had attempted a comeback in February. Delegates from the country had come to Prague by train, by car and truck, on bicycles and by every means of transport imaginable.

Now they were given workers' overalls and documents showing that they were employed at the factory in Vysočany. Well-known politicians who were in danger of being recognized and arrested were bundled into ambulances and, accompanied by doctors, hurried to the factory's first aid station. The Workers' Militia protectively surrounded the whole district while the Congress was sitting.

Out of 1,543 elected delegates, 1,192 attended the Congress. Except for the majority of Slovaks, whose journey to Prague was prevented by occupation units, and a handful of conservatives, who under the circumstances thought it unwise to attend, the presence of a quorum guaranteed the legality of the proceedings. The Congress sat late into the evening under strictly conspiratorial conditions. It proclaimed its sitting to be a permanent one and issued a political proclamation sharply condemning the intervention. An appeal was addressed to all Communist and workers' parties throughout the world, condemning the Soviet Union for destroying the fundamentals of proletarian internationalism and asking help in the struggle to restore the sovereignty of a small state. An appeal to the Slovak nation was drafted, as well as a letter to Alexander Dubček and the other arrested, kidnaped Party leaders. Then the Congress elected a Central Committee, headed by Alexander Dubček and other noted representatives of the Party's progressive wing. Late that night, the new Central Committee of the Communist Party of Czechoslovakia elected its Presidium and secretariat.

While the Extraordinary Congress was in session, President Svoboda demanded direct negotiations, in Moscow, with Soviet leaders. In a short radio announcement he said he was leaving for Moscow the next day to try to resolve the difficult crisis in which the state found itself. Svoboda would be accompanied by the Minister of National Defense, General Dzúr; the Deputy Premier, Dr. Husák; the Minister of Justice, Dr. Kučera (representing non-Communist parties in the National Front); and by three well-known conservatives: Indra, Bilák and Kolder. The government and the National Assembly gave full authority to accompany the President to only the first three politicians, ostentatiously ignoring the three traitors.

On Friday, August 23, Svoboda arrived in Moscow with his entourage. He was welcomed by many prominent Soviet representatives; Soviet television attempted to insinuate a cordial interpretation of the welcome by shots of kisses and embraces. It had to use old pictures, however, because Svoboda refused to embrace those who had treacherously attacked his country. At the beginning of negotiations in the Kremlin, Svoboda categorically insisted that the kidnaped Czechoslovak politicians must participate. The Soviet leaders had to capitulate, even though the Soviet press had meanwhile branded Dubček a traitor, having written that he usurped Party leadership and was backed by only a minority of the Presidium which he had made a majority by terror. Beyond doubt, Svoboda's courage and firmness led to this Soviet capitulation, but the political bankruptcy of the occupation and news of the single-minded resistance of the people also played a part.

Accordingly, on Saturday, August 24, Dubček, Černík, Smrkovský and Kriegel were taken to Moscow. They had spent forty-eight hours in an underground retreat in the Carpathian mountains, without food or drink, handcuffed and isolated. Moscow had been forced to make the first concession: to recognize as partners men it had branded as traitors (and for whom a political trial was obviously being prepared).

In Prague, the new Central Committee learned of the negotiations in Moscow, and also that the Russians had been forced to release the arrested leaders. The Central Committee knew that in order to divert the ridicule created by the successful meeting of the Extraordinary Congress, *Pravda* had stated that the Congress was an illegal assembly of revisionists. The new Central Committee believed it was of paramount importance, come what may, to inform the comrades who had been kidnaped on the night of the occupation of the nation's unanimous resistance. Dubček needed to know of the Extraordinary Congress, and of the fact that the whole people backed them as its representatives had never been backed before. They decided to send a delegation from the new Central Committee to Moscow. Ambassador Chervonenko insisted that conservative members of the old Presidium should go as well.

The Moscow negotiations were very difficult. Again the Soviet politicians employed open threats that, this time, were specific: The Czechoslovak Republic would be liquidated as an independent state; Slovakia would become a federated Soviet Republic and Bohemia an autonomous territory. The Czechoslovak intellectuals would be deported to Siberia and a strict military regime installed. Were these threats serious? The Czechoslovak leaders realized that men who were able to attack an ally treacherously, by night, were capable of anything. After all, a fate similar to theirs had overtaken the Baltic states.

The Czech and Slovak representatives knew that their own lives and the nation's life were at stake. In the debates and personal quarrels there were heartbreaking scenes. A Moscow Protocol was finally signed, containing fifteen secret points and a public communiqué. Moscow was once again compelled to recognize Dubček as First Secretary of the Party and Černík as Premier. To Černík's parting question about what should be done with the potential collaborators who were with them, Brezhnev replied that they should take them back to Prague and do with them what they thought fit. The traitors were no longer of any value to their protectors. Indra collapsed on hearing this—a heart attack in the moment of fear? He remained in Moscow for treatment.

The Czechoslovak representatives were forced to sign promises that the Fourteenth Congress would not be recognized as legal, that they would reintroduce censorship, and that all clubs and political organizations that had sprung up outside the framework of the National Front would be dissolved. They would undertake no change in foreign policy. In return, the armies of occupation would gradually be recalled as the normalization of conditions was established. But Moscow would be the sole judge of whether "normalization" had indeed been achieved.

The Czechoslovaks signed a promise that they would work to strengthen friendship between the Soviet peoples and the nation whose feelings had been so deeply wounded. They also had to accept a list of people unacceptable to the Soviets who were to retire from political life. The Soviet Union, for its part, promised to recognize the post-January development and not to interfere in internal affairs.

Very shortly before their departure for Prague, the Czechoslovaks were offered friendly help in preparing a political trial against "Zionists and counterrevolutionists," wherein Dr. Kriegel and Dr. Goldstuecker, the chairman of the Writers' Union, would figure prominently. President Svoboda stated that if the Soviets insisted on the trial he would cancel his signature to the protocols. When their friendly service was so stubbornly rejected, the Russians no longer insisted on keeping Kriegel in Moscow. He was allowed to leave for Prague with his friends, on condition that he give up political activity.

Early on Tuesday, August 27, the delegation finally returned to Prague. In the hours after the Moscow communiqué had been made public, President Svoboda and Alexander Dubček spoke movingly on the radio. Several times, Dubček's speech was suddenly interrupted when he became unwell and had to be helped by a doctor. The following day, equally moving speeches were made by Premier Černík and by the chairman of the National Assembly, Josef Smrkovský. The tortured Czechoslovak people learned of Moscow's conditions. They learned, too, of their leaders' determination to continue with the rejuvenating process—only under more complicated and difficult conditions, and far more slowly than had been originally intended. The Czech and Slovak nations, after initial hesitation, expressed confidence in their leaders.

The Czechoslovak Spring was over. It had begun with the January revolt of the Party's Central Committee and matured in the spread of popular activity and the realization of "socialism with a human face." It had blossomed in heroic national resistance during the first week of the occupation, and now it was finished.

The second part of the despairing battle has begun. In the presence of an occupying army, under the relentless pressure of occupying powers, the people are resolved to surrender none of their longing. By their determination to preserve their own sovereignty and to show the world that it is possible to unite socialism and democracy, they want to continue the fight for a better future, not only for themselves, but for everyone.

Afterword: February 1969

Six months have passed since the military intervention of August 21, 1968, but the "controlled revolution" in the Socialist Republic of Czechoslovakia is not over. The Czechoslovakian people continue to fight for "socialism with a human face." The Czechoslovakian question remains one of the chief problems of international politics.

The perspective of six months makes it easier to see why the Soviet Union decided upon a course that violated international law, almost led to a resumption of the Cold War, and supplied anti-Communist propagandists with excellent arguments. Not only were grave problems created for the international proletarian movement by the intervention, but the Soviet Union was forced into isolation.

Today it is clear that the intervention was not the result of strategic considerations. Czechoslovakia did not resign from the Warsaw Pact, nor was she interested in neutrality. Neither West Germany nor the United States considered intervening to aid a "Czechoslovakian counterrevolution." Under the terms of the agreement forced upon Czechoslovakia for "temporary stationing of Warsaw Pact troops," Soviet troops remaining in the country are stationed a great distance from the Bavarian border, which is still guarded solely by Czechoslovakian units. The placement of Soviet garrisons mainly in Moravia and Slovakia is the best evidence for assuming that concern for the security of the western border of the socialist bloc was only a pretext. (A Czech joke goes that Czechoslovakia made an unbelievably profitable exchange: for "Two Thousand Words" she got six thousand tanks.)

Nor was the main reason for intervention a Soviet fear that the freedom of press and assembly that had been proclaimed in Czechoslovakia might spread to other socialist countries. Certainly this freedom was inflammatory and threatened gradually to become a great danger to centralism as conceived by the Soviets. But informed sources explain that this was not a decisive factor.

The main cause of the intervention was, rather, the danger that Czechoslovakia would free herself from the strict control that the Soviet regime had exercised for twenty years, which Moscow's bureaucrats considered the most important guarantee of their influence. All connections between the Soviet regime and the Czechoslovakian state security forces, the intelligence organization, the Army, and the Party apparatus were in danger of being destroyed. During the "Prague Spring," the vassals of Moscow were removed from all these institutions and replaced by individuals whom the Soviets did not know and whose obedience was not assured.

The planned Fourteenth Party Congress was to have chosen a new Central Committee whose members would by no means have had Moscow's blessing. This Party Congress, which haunted the Soviet regime like a nightmare, seems to have been the immediate cause for the entry of a half million soldiers into Czechoslovakia. This obviously encouraged the Soviets to behave like the worst imperialistic aggressor.

The invasion became a political issue of the first order, wherein the heroic resistance of the entire population and the courage of the leading politicians frustrated the imposition of a quisling regime. Though Moscow was forced to allow the arrested "traitorous" leaders to return to Prague, the Soviet regime successfully accomplished the chief purpose of its intervention. One after another, the boldest proponents of the new socialist model were compelled to resign their positions in the leadership, to be replaced by vassals of Moscow. During negotiations in the Kremlin in August, František Kriegel, chairman of the National Front; Ota Šik, acting head of the government; Josef Pavel, the Minister of the Interior; and Jiří Hájek, the Foreign Minister, were relieved of their posts. In the months that followed, Dr. Zdeněk Mlynář was removed from the Party Presidium, followed later by Vladimír Kadlec, the Minister of Education. The flagrant traitors and collaborators Bilák and Indra were able to re-enter the Party Presidium, although they had lost their following.

The men who had to give up their jobs in the spring and summer of 1968 are returning to the state security police and the intelligence service. Generals accused of defending in August the true political foundations of the "Prague Spring" are being forced to leave the Army.

The Fourteenth Party Congress, which met on August 22, 1968, under the protection of Prague workers and under the noses of the occupying powers, was declared invalid under pressure from Moscow. It will probably be permitted to meet again only after the election of new delegates; in this way, it is hoped that as many conservatives and dogmatists as possible will be salvaged for the next Central Committee.

The establishment of a Czech Communist Party became essential after the Declaration of Federalization, because of the existence of an independent Slovakian Communist Party. Under Soviet pressure, this too has been postponed indefinitely; a so-called "Office for the Czech States" has been substituted, under the chairmanship of Lubomír Štrougal, a man who will do anything to win the Soviets' trust.

Now that Moscow has re-established internal control in the security, Army, and Party apparatuses, her main purpose is to leave the dirty work of erasing the gains of the Prague Spring to precisely those men whom the Spring brought leadership. Men who have earned a world-wide reputation and become symbols of the renewal of socialism must now assume the tasks imposed by the relentless pressure of the Soviet regime.

Thus it can be maintained that nothing has happened, and Soviet attempts to achieve cooperation with the United States— unavoidable in the light of China's increasing activity in world politics—can be resumed. The Soviet theory of "limited sovereignty," which encountered vehement resistance everywhere (but especially in Rumania, Yugoslavia, and the Communist parties of the West)—this theory can now simply be shelved until it is needed again. Thus it will once again be possible for the Soviets to present a friendly face to the world.

It must be confirmed that, in this respect, Moscow has already achieved some success.

The majority of Party functionaries and of the Czechoslovak population acted together against the occupiers on August 21 (with the exception of the traitors, who thus lost all their prestige and support in the Party and among the people). But within a few months the situation had changed. The intrigues and threats of Moscow as well as the exertions of the Soviet emissary Kusnetzov, who was sent to Prague because Ambassador Chervonenko had behaved impossibly (he remains for the present in Czechoslovakia only for reasons of prestige), have brought to the fore a number of men who are ready not only to collaborate but to force the popular leaders to change their positions.

After the August "negotiations" in Moscow, the Central Committee was enlarged by eighty progressive members, all of whom took part in the "illegal" Fourteenth Party Congress. Nevertheless, the conservative bloc inside and outside the Central Committee is extraordinarily active, thanks to material and moral support from the occupying troops. This bloc, ignoring the Party statutes that presently obtain, maintains strict discipline within the faction, calls conferences, prints illegal pamphlets, organizes campaigns, etc. Members work unanimously in Central Committee meetings and seek to influence negotiations with the Soviets.

On the other hand, most of the new, progressive members of the Central Committee are never able to get the floor—

whether out of fear, lack of experience, naïve insistence on the letter of the statutes, or insistence on democratic rules of order. Today it is officially admitted that anti-socialist forces were on the verge of organizing in August and that the Party was incapable of hindering this development. Today we hear that the unity of the Party and of socialism is endangered, above all by "anti-socialist," "right-wing," "opportunistic-liberal" forces—which the intelligentsia lead. Thus the August occupation is styled a "misunderstanding" that must be cleared up by intensifying Czechoslovakia's relations with the occupying countries.

What remains of the Prague Spring?

Today everyone from the most crass Stalinist to the most unbending progressive professes faith in the principles of the Prague Spring. Moscow has written off Novotný and his most intimate associates.

Czech-Slovak federalization must be uncomfortable for the Soviets because of the neighboring Ukraine; nevertheless, it has been achieved, although not within the Party. The rehabilitation of victims of political trials continues. Laws are being drafted that will supposedly guarantee the democratization of the courts. But one hardly supposes that a truly autonomous bench can be assured, as has recently been promised by the regime. Probably a few measures will be preserved in order to guarantee that the government really governs, that the National Assembly makes laws, and that the parties and organizations of the National Front are more than mere paper agencies of the Communist Party.

Freedom of assembly and freedom to form organizations, two of the most important achievements of the Prague Spring, are now considerably restricted. Independent clubs have been dissolved. Freedom of the press has suffered most—although the press, radio, and television in Czechoslovakia remain the freest mass media in the socialist world. Again and again, attempts have been made to restrict free speech, but these have encountered unanimous resistance from the public, the journalists and artists. So far, the reintroduction of pre-publication censorship has been prevented. The press and television—less so the radio—remain a forum for criticism and polemics; they are a check on the rulers and a force for partriotism, freedom and democracy. Only time will show how long they can keep a measure of independence in the face of constant threats.

Doubtless the present regime deserves praise for not having persecuted anyone because of his political convictions or activities in the months before August 21, although there has been a numerical increase in Stalinist members of the police who are loyal to Moscow.

The weak economy, the sinking morale of the workers, and especially the ceaseless Stalinist attacks from the Warsaw Pact states make it difficult to implement the economic reform. This reform remains a part of the government's program, but is considered revisionist, especially in the German Democratic Republic. Nevertheless, the reform continues to be debated, parts of it are being put into effect, and in the near future the National Assembly is supposed to pass laws concerning the independence of industries and Workers' Councils. It is precisely these Workers' Councils that could form the foundation of a socialist democracy.

It is crucial to the future of Czechoslovakia that a return to pure Stalinism or a "Kádárization" of the country, wherein the people vegetate in an apathetic atmosphere under a more or less liberal regime, be prevented. The most important factor in forestalling such developments is the important changes that have occurred in both parts of the Republic: Slovakia and the Czech states.

Federalization has been completed in Slovakia, which is now an independent state. In addition, the legal Congress of the Slovakian Communist Party took place on August 26, 1968. Federalization led to a nationalistic euphoria. Gustav Husák, the man who deserves most of the credit for the foundation of an independent Slovakian republic within the framework of the federation, now has unlimited authority in Slovakia and enjoys the highest popularity in the Party.* He has been able to ensure his absolute control over the party and to remove all conservatives from the Party apparatus. Bilák, a symbol of treason and collaboration, was not even chosen for the Slovak Central Committee, and it is only by Moscow's grace that he still sits in the Party Presidium in Prague.

However, Husák himself, a man of such great ability that he towers above his colleagues in Bratislava and Prague alike, has demonstrably undergone no further political or intellectual development since 1951, the date of his imprisonment. He is a Communist of the old type; for him, the Soviet Union, despite events, remains the incarnation of socialism. For him, Lenin's theses—in large part Stalin's interpretations—are still the most important guide. Thus Husák has gradually become the spokesman of the neo-conservative wing of the Central Committee: all severe measures to limit civil liberties come from him; he is the chief representative of the "realistic" approach that labels the August occupation a "misunderstanding" and calls for a battle against "anti-socialist forces." Practically speaking, all Slovakia stands behind Husák, the father of the Slovakian nationalist movement.

In Slovakia, the only political alternative to Husák is the bankrupt Bilák. As long as the present nationalistic euphoria continues, Slovakia under Husák will remain a conservative factor in further developments. But the fact that August 21 effected an extraordinary strengthening of the bonds between Czechs and Slovaks allows one to hope that this euphoria will not endure.

The incredible fact is that the entire population refuses to recognize the reality of the occupation: in the Czech states *that* is the most important reality. Eight months of the Prague Spring and the first week of heroic resistance against the occupying powers have left an ineradicable mark upon the people's consciousness. Nothing can daunt their democratic unity or their determination to struggle for the ideals of democratic

---

* Husák became First Secretary of the entire Czechoslovak Party in April 1969, replacing Dubček. Ed.

socialism: neither the presence of foreign troops nor the constant Soviet propaganda, neither the recent activity of Stalinist shock troops (given all possible support by Moscow) nor the appeals of state and Party leaders who threaten "incalculable consequences" and a national catastrophe if the "reality" of events since August is not accepted.

This determination is most marked in the unanimity of the working class, who had been hesitant before August. The breach of trust by their Soviet friends during the occupation horrified and shook them so much that a profound change of opinion occurred. Since then the working class has been the chief proponent of "socialism with a human face."

The workers insist upon their demands for democratic justice. They demand the realization of the economic reform that earlier they feared. The workers elect Workers' Councils in the factories; to prove their maturity, they also choose technicians and economic experts who guarantee cooperation with management. The unions, for twenty years the bulwark of Novotný's brand of bureaucracy, have transformed themselves into the most important organization of progressive energies in Czech society. The Metalworkers' Union, with almost a million members, has become the especial avant-garde of the ideas of the Prague Spring.

Students and youth back the working class. During the August days young people displayed much civil courage and patriotism. Now they are the firm friends of the workers. The four-day student strike in November 1968 first demonstrated mass resistance against the "reality" of the collaborators and was successful only because the working class stood solidly behind the students. Lasting contacts grew up between the factories and the universities. The heroic act of Jan Palach deeply shocked the entire population. Student demonstrations after his death and burial were the strongest manifestations of popular opinion since May Day, 1968.

But it is true that weariness is already noticeable. For more than a year, Czechoslovakians have lived in an atmosphere of unprecedented political activity—and theirs is the most intense political engagement in the world. The distribution of illegal Stalinist pamphlets full of crude insults and threats only aggravates the situation. The "incalculable consequences" of which the leaders speak in order to calm the political climate are threatening enough—if one is familiar with Czechoslovakia's partners and their methods—that no one doubts their reality.

Thus, political euphoria and enthusiasm for the newly achieved solidarity and activity daily alternate with deep depression. This depression springs from the knowledge that nothing is impossible and that no one will aid Czechoslovakia in case of catastrophe. Weariness is useful to the Stalinists and neo-conservatives who wish for nothing more than a funeral calm and general apathy—even for the decay of the Party, into whose place a small, exclusive, sectarian, and obedient Communist Party organization could then step.

In July 1968, Dubček said that you have to change the leaders if you can't change the people. The Stalinist and neo-conservatives want to cripple the people, to give them a feeling of powerlessness and force them at last to be submissive. They have remained unsuccessful in this attempt, although Moscow supports them with all her power. They remain unsuccessful, although the center of the Party leadership—which has only the unity and courage of the people to thank that it has remained in power and, indeed, alive—now retreats step by step under the pressure of foreign and internal forces, and thereby lowers itself into an alliance with the neo-conservatives.

Nevertheless, these leaders still have the people's trust. If someone today tried to remove Svoboda or Dubček, he would probably have a general strike on his hands. Will this be true tomorrow? Will unheard-of pressure and the threats of violence to which the leaders are exposed succeed in "changing the people," in making them fall into lethargy and passivity?

That is the decisive question for Czechoslovakia in the second year of her great awakening that has shaken the world and brought new hope for socialism and democracy.

Chronology

1952

Trials of Rudolf Slánský and others

1953

Novotný comes to power; Stalinist "iron and steel" concept of centrally directed extensive economic development fully adopted

1954

"Slovak nationalists" sentenced to long prison terms

1960

New constitution for Slovakia

1961

22nd Congress of Soviet Communist Party

1963

"Barnabitky" Commission appointed by the Central Committee to examine prison sentences dating from trials in fifties, especially those of Novomeský and Husák
Ota Šik's proposal for economic reform: "intensive development"

1966

13th Congress of Czechoslovakian Communist Party adopts Šik's reform; *Reportér* (Journalists' Union weekly) is born

1967

June

4th Congress of Writers' Union: open conflict between writers and Party leadership, centering on position regarding Arab-Israeli conflict

Summer

Novotný increases Slovak-Czech tension on visit to Rybarpole and Martin

September

Central Committee of Czechoslovak Party meets and expels from Party writers Vaculík, Klíma and Liehm

October

Central Committee plenum: open criticism of Novotný

October 30

Students of Strahov hostel, Prague, attacked by police, who misinterpreted their demonstration at Hradčany Castle; enormous public reaction against Party leadership

December

Central Committee turns against Novotný and conservatives

1968

January 4

Committee reconvenes; Novotný is attacked and resigns as First Secretary; housing shortage of most concern to many Czechs

January 6

Dubček elected First Secretary of Communist Party; for first time, leader elected by full Central Committee of 100, not by 14-man Presidium

January 21

Smrkovský in a speech says that the people should be informed of all official activities through news media; signal for increased journalistic liberty

January 22
Jiří Hendrych remains the most formidable conservative on Central Committee; he tries without success to prevent dissemination of uncensored news

January 26
General Jan Šejna scandal: official accusation after Šejna's flight to the Americans via Rome

February 25
20th anniversary celebration of Czechoslovak Party in power

February 27
News of Šejna affair breaks and is linked to alleged plot to keep Novotný in power; warrant for his arrest is issued

March 1
Literární noviny, formerly under tight rein of Ministry of Culture (Hendrych), becomes *Literární listy* in protest against attempts to muzzle press.

March 5
Hendrych dismissed as Party Secretary for ideological matters
Public panels: revelations about fifties trials and political crimes

March 7
Pilgrimage to Jan Masaryk's grave becomes a political demonstration

March 14
East German newspapers open fire on Czech reforms

March 16
Prague censors at Central Publications office publish resolution saying they want to quit

March 22
Novotný resigns as President

March 23
Dresden conference of five Warsaw Pact states (excluding Rumania); Dubček attends

March 26
Dubček gives press conference for 134 writers

March 28
Svoboda chosen as President despite popular call for Čestmír Císár

April
Action Program unanimously approved by Central Committee; Dubček's famous speech calling for "socialism with a human face"

New political clubs emerge (K231, Kan)

April 3
Czech national student organization demands investigation of circumstances of Jan Masaryk's death

April 5
Plenum: New, smaller (11-man) Presidium elected by secret ballot; media present

April 6
Josef Lenárt government resigns; as Premier, Oldřich Černík forms new government

April 26
Budapest meeting with Soviet and other East European Parties to plan World Communist conference for November 1968; half of Parties absent; Lenárt heads Czech delegation

May
May Day Celebration characterized by spontaneity and informality; estimated 140,000 Czechs crowd the streets, not in formal review

May 5
Soviet Presidium meets in Moscow: Dubček, Černík, Smrkovský and Bilák present

Warsaw press opens attack on Czech reforms

May 6
Central Committee session: 150th anniversary of Marx's birthday

May 18
Kosygin comes to Karlovy Vary and is optimistic about outcome of

Czechoslovak Central Committee session; Soviet Defense Minister Marshal Grechko in Prague with mission to plan June maneuvers of Warsaw Pact armies
Czech Parliament sends delegation to tour USSR

May 22
Tito praises Czech reforms

May 30
Central Committee meeting: Dubček announces Extraordinary Czechoslovakian Party Congress for September

June 1
Soviet troops first enter Slovakia for maneuvers

June 11
Czech reforms spur Hungarian demands; Kádár reported positive toward Czech developments

June 19
Workers' Militia (conservative) meets at Ruzyně Airport with Dubček

June 19–30
Warsaw Pact armies engage in maneuvers, commanded by Marshal Yakubovsky

Mid-June
District Party conferences meet all over Czechoslovakia
Wildcat strikes not approved by official trade union organization

June 26
National Assembly meets, relaxes press law (i.e. censorship) and passes rehabilitation law including compensation for years in prison

June 27
The "Two Thousand Words" published in *Literární listy*

June 28
Presidium condemns "Two Thousand Words" as counterrevolutionary (only, subsequently, to reverse this position)

July 10
Special Assembly session; Čestmír Císař elected chairman of Czech National Council

July 15
General Václav Prchlík affair: the general angers Moscow

July 18
Radio broadcast of Warsaw Five's letter to Czech leadership

July 19
Central Committee meets at Hradčany; Dubček reassures people of his faith in a just socialism and in reforms

July 20–29
Moscow's *Pravda* reports discovery of arms, allegedly belonging to anti-Dubček counterrevolutionaries, at Cheb (near German border); publishes piece emphasizing Czechs' economic dependence; warns "time is running out"

July 29
Bilateral meeting between USSR and Czechoslovakia at Čierná nad Tisou

July 26–August 1
Literární listy publishes an appeal to Presidium written by Pavel Kohout

August 2
Pragovka factory workers send letter to *Pravda* expressing their conservative fears

August 3
Bratislava meeting of Warsaw Pact states
Tito visits Czechoslovakia and is warmly welcomed
Ulbricht visits Karlovy Vary for amiable meeting with Czech leaders

August 17
Pravda breaks three-week silence with piece accusing Czech press of slander

August 20
Central Committee Presidium meets; plans for Fourteenth, Extraordinary Congress
Warsaw Pact armies cross Czechoslovakian borders about 11 P.M.
Central Committee decides in early hours of August 21 to issue proclamation appealing for peaceful resistance

August 21
Central Committee appeal read on Prague Radio
Top politicians arrested by Soviet troops in early hours of 21st

August 21–27
National Assembly meets in unbroken session under siege; Svoboda called upon at Hradčany by potential members of Soviet-sponsored government

August 22
Fourteenth, Extraordinary Congress meets clandestinely in Vysočany factory, outside Prague

August 23
Svoboda arrives in Moscow with his cabinet

August 24
Dubček, Černík, Smrkovský and Kriegel released and allowed to participate in Moscow negotiations

1969

January 26
Hero's funeral in Prague for Jan Palach, student who burned himself to death in protest against occupation

February
Growing strength of conservatives, though Dubček and other leaders permitted to stay on

February 27
Brezhnev confers with Czech Defense Minister Martin Dzúr

March 4
7th Czech Trade Union Congress opens, supports Workers' Council legislation opposed by Soviets

March 13
Gustav Husák, Slovak Party Secretary, dismisses Miroslav Kusy, chief ideological secretary and a liberal toward reforms

March 19
Joint military staff to be inaugurated for Warsaw Pact; Dubček chairs

Warsaw Pact meeting at Budapest, showing Soviets' apparent confidence in "normalization" of Czechoslovakia

April 2
Press censorship restored; Marshal Grechko visits Prague

April 8–9
Presidium of Czechoslovakian Party approves inquiry into journalism; newsmen summoned to hearings from major dailies and weeklies

April 14
Dubček visits Moscow; public reacts to news of more Soviet troops (an announcement later rescinded) and to dropping of liberals from Presidium

April 17
January to April campaign against Josef Smrkovský, who is widely popular to the point of becoming a symbol of resistance, concludes as he concedes political error and is dropped from the Presidium
Alexander Dubček ousted as First Secretary and replaced by Gustav Husák at Presidium meeting

Bibliography

GENERAL

České dějiny [Bohemian History]. A multi-volumed history begun in Prague in 1912 by the prominent historian Václav Novotný, and projected to cover Czech history from earliest times to the twentieth century. By 1966, fourteen volumes had been published, covering up to the year 1464. The enterprise is now directed by the Historical Institute of the Czechoslovak Academy of Sciences.

Heymann, Frederick G. *Poland and Czechoslovakia.* Englewood Cliffs, N.J.: Prentice-Hall, Spectrum Books, 1966.

Lettrich, Josef. *History of Modern Slovakia.* New York: Praeger, 1955.

Rechcígl, Miloslav, ed. *The Czechoslovak Contribution to World Culture.* The Hague: Mouton, for the Czechoslovak Society of Arts and Sciences in America, 1964. Fifty-three contributors, of whom forty-four were born in Czechoslovakia, writing on contributions to all cultural fields by Czechs and Slovaks.

Seton-Watson, R. W. *A History of the Czechs and Slovaks.* 2d ed. London: Shoe String Press, 1965.

Thomson, Samuel H. *Czechoslovakia in European History.* 2d ed. Princeton University Press, 1953.

15TH–16TH CENTURIES

Macek, Josef. *The Hussite Movement in Bohemia.* 2d ed. Prague: Orbis, 1958.

Spinka, Matthew. *John Hus's Concept of the Church*. Princeton University Press, 1966.

17TH–18TH CENTURIES

Kerner, Robert J. *Bohemia in the Eighteenth Century*. New York: Macmillan, 1932.

Sommer, Ernest. *Into Exile: The History of the Counter-Reformation in Bohemia, 1620–1650*. London: New Europe Publishing Co., 1943.

19TH–20TH CENTURIES

Beneš, Eduard. *My War Memoirs*. Boston: Houghton, 1928.

———. *From Munich to New War and New Victory*. Boston: Houghton, 1954.

Čapek, Karel. *President Masaryk Tells His Story*. London: G. Allen, 1934. Dialogues with Tomáš G. Masaryk, conducted by Czechoslovakia's leading twentieth-century writer.

Craig, Gordon, and F. Gilbert, eds. *The Diplomats, 1919–1939*. Princeton University Press, 1953.

Eliáš, Zdeněk, and Jaromír Netík, "Czechoslovakia." In *Communism in Europe*, ed. William E Griffith, vol. 2. Cambridge, Mass.: M.I.T. Press, 1953.

Kann, Robert. *The Multinational Empire: Nationalism and National Reform in the Habsburg Monarchy, 1848–1918*. 2 volumes. New York: Columbia University Press, 1950.

Kerner, Robert J., ed. *Czechoslovakia: Twenty Years of Independence*. Berkeley: University of California Press, 1940.

Mamatey, Victor S. *The United States and East Central Europe: A Study of Wilsonian Diplomacy and Propaganda*. Princeton University Press, 1957.

Masaryk, Tomáš G. *The Spirit of Russia.* 2 vols. New York: Macmillan, 1919.

––––––. *The New Europe.* New York: 1918.

––––––. *The Making of a State.* London: Allen & Underwood, 1927.

Perman, D. *The Shaping of the Czechoslovak State: Diplomatic History of the Boundaries of Czechoslovakia, 1914–1920.* Leiden: Brill, 1962.

Seton-Watson, Hugh. *Eastern Europe between the Wars.* Cambridge University Press, 1945.

Seton-Watson, R. W., ed. *Slovakia Then and Now: A Political Survey.* London: G. Allen, 1931. Essays by leading Slovaks.

Wheeler-Bennett, John W. *Munich: Prologue to Tragedy.* New York: Duell, 1948.

Wiskemann, Elizabeth. *Czechs and Germans.* London: Oxford University Press, 1938.

POST-WORLD WAR II

Chapman, Colin. *August 21st: The Rape of Czechoslovakia.* Philadelphia: Lippincott, 1968. Dispatches by foreign editors, *The Sunday Times* (London).

Ello, Paul, ed. *Czechoslovakia's Blueprint for Freedom: Dubček's Unity, Socialism, and Humanity Statements—the Original and Official Documents Leading to the Conflict of August 1968.* Washington D.C.: Acropolis Books, 1968. Includes complete text of the 1968 Action Program of the Communist Party of Czechoslovakia.

Kohák, Erazim V. "Requiem for Utopia," *Dissent* (Winter 1968), pp. 41–48.

Korbel, Josef. *The Communist Subversion of Czechoslovakia, 1938–1948.* Princeton University Press, 1961.

Littell, Robert, ed. *The Czech Black Book.* New York: Praeger, 1969.

The New York Times, January 1, 1968–September 1, 1969. Dispatches by David Binder, Robert C. Doty, Richard Eder, Clyde Farnsworth, Peter Grose, Bernard Gwertzman, Paul Hofmann, Henry Kamm, Jonathan Randal, Henry Raymont, Dana Adams Schmidt, Harry Schwartz, Alvin Shuster, and Tad Szulc.

Schwartz, Harry. *Prague's 200 Days: The Struggle for Democracy in Czechoslovakia.* New York: Praeger, 1969.

Seton-Watson, Hugh, ed. *Nationalism and Communism.* New York: Praeger, 1964.

Šik, Ota. *Plan and Market under Socialism.* New York: International Arts and Sciences Press, 1967.

Táborský, Edward. *Communism in Czechoslovakia, 1948–1960.* Princeton University Press, 1961.

Zeman, Z. A. B. *Prague Spring 1968.* London: Penguin, 1969.

Zinner, Paul E. *Communist Strategy and Tactics in Czechoslovakia, 1918–1948.* New York: Praeger, 1963.

MODERN LITERATURE

Čapek, Karel. *War with the Newts.* New York: Berkley Medallion Books.

———. *R U R.* In *Contemporary Drama: 9 Plays* (*1941*), eds. E. Bradlee Watson and Benfield Pressey. New York: Scribner. The 1921 drama that introduced "robot" to the modern vocabulary.

Hašek, Jaroslav. *The Good Soldier Schweik.* New York: Ungar, 1963; also New American Library Signet Books.

Havel, Václav. *The Memorandum* and *Garden Party.* Plays. New York: Grove Evergreen Books, 1967.

Index

Bacílek, Karel, 19
Banská Bystrica, 19
Beneš, Eduard, 17, 18, 50, 57, 58, 67, 133
Berlin, 10, 92, 94, 159
Bilák, Vasil, 88–90, 94, 95, 108, 173, 180, 184
Bonn, 28
Bratislava, 19, 40, 100, 125, 126, 146
Brezhnev, Leonid, 36, 37, 146, 154, 169
Brno, 36, 86, 124

Čapek, Karel, 5
Ceaucescu, Nicolae, 132, 153, 155
Čepička, Dr. Alexei, 59, 60
Černík, Oldřich, 39, 64, 65, 94, 98, 102, 119, 158, 161, 170, 171, 174, 175, 176
Cheb, 140
Chervonenko, Stepan Vassilievitch, 161, 169, 175, 181
Chop, 145
Chudík, Michal, 35
Čierná nad Tisou, 142–52, 155, 157
Císař, Čestmír, 6, 57, 86, 95–97, 124, 161–62

David, Václav, 38
Dubček, Alexander, 34, 35, 39, 40, 42–45, 48, 61–64, 77, 85, 86, 87, 88–90, 92, 94, 95, 98, 99,
103, 105–7, 119, 121, 133, 137–40, 141, 146, 149, 150, 157, 158, 162, 173–76, 186
Dzúr, General Martin, 44, 97

Fierlinger, Zdeněk, 170
Fischer, Ernst, 4
Franz, Joseph I, 26
Fromm, Erich, 4

Galicia, 88
Goldstuecker, Eduard, 7, 42, 76, 83, 115, 176
Gomułka, Władysław, 43, 93
Gorki, 62
Gottwald, Klement, 31, 49, 50, 59, 65, 66
Gramsci, Antonio, 4
Grechko, Marshal Andrei, 97

Hager, Professor Kurt, 94, 130
Hájek, Jiří, 180
Hanzelka, Jiří, 7, 124
Havel, Václav, 5
Hearst, William Randolph, 28
Hejzlar, Josef, 49
Hendrych, Jiří, 6, 26, 28, 34, 38, 41, 46, 140
Herder, Johann Gottfried, 17
Hofmann, Karel, 160–61
Hradec-Králové, 36
Hus, Jan, 16
Husák, Dr. Gustav, 4, 19, 20, 107, 125, 126, 173, 183, 184

Indra, Alois, 87, 90, 119, 121, 157, 170, 173, 180
Interhelpo, 62
Israel, 25

Janko, General, 45
Jodas, Josef, 115
Johnson, Lyndon B., 160

Kádár, János, 92, 183
Kadlec, Vladimír, 180
Kafka, Franz, 5
Karlovy Vary, 97, 154
Karvaš, Peter, 5
Khrushchev, Nikita S., 2, 60, 97
Kirghiz SSR, 61
Klíma, Ivan, 26, 28
Kodaj, General Samuel, 118, 171
Köhler, Bruno, 88
Kohout, Pavel, 5, 28, 124, 142
Kolder, Drahomír, 87, 90, 140, 157, 173
Konstantinov, G., 96
Košice, 19, 66, 142
Kosík, Karel, 3
Kosygin, Aleksei N., 97, 147
Koucký, Vladimír, 6
Kriegel, Dr. František, 86, 146, 162, 174–76, 180
Kučera, Dr. Bohuslav, 173
Kulturný život, 6, 24, 42, 125
Kundera, Milan, 26, 28
Kusnetzov, 181

Lány, 55
Le Monde, 97
Lenárt, Josef, 39, 68
Lenin, Nikolai, 64
Lidová demokracie, 53
Liehm, Antonín J., 26, 28
Literární listy, 46, 47, 52, 98, 117, 142
Literární noviny, 3, 6, 24–26, 28, 46
Lomský, General Bohumír, 171
Longo, Luigi, 160

Macháčová, Božena, 170
Mamula, Miroslav, 35, 130

Marcuse, Herbert, 4
Martin, 21
Marx, Karl, 64, 94–96
Masaryk, Jan, 58, 84
Masaryk, Tomáš Garrigue, 9, 17, 57, 84
Matica Slovenská, 21
Milovice, 100
Mladá fronta, 97, 120
Mlynář, Zdeněk, 42, 180
Moravec, Colonel Jaroslav, 44
Moscow, 35, 50, 54, 64, 65, 67, 92, 94, 129, 141, 160, 174, 175, 179–85, 186
Munich, 94, 133, 143, 149, 151

Neues Deutschland, 129, 159
Novomeský, Ladislav, 4, 19, 20
Novotný, Antonín, 1=4, 7–8, 14–15, 20–22, 25, 27–28, 30=45, 51, 53, 57, 60, 62–64, 65, 68, 71, 75–77, 83, 84, 85–88, 90, 92, 98, 102, 103, 105–7, 112, 113, 129, 138=40, 167, 171, 182, 185

Ostrava, 20, 36, 64, 87, 90, 114

Palach, Jan, 185
Paris, 28
Pavel, Josef, 168, 180
Pavlíček, František, 5
Pavlovský, Oldřich, 170
Plojhar, Josef, 53
Práce, 42, 48, 53
Prague, 19, 20, 48, 66, 67, 92, 94, 97, 117, 138, 145, 147, 154, 160, 162, 168, 172, 173, 176, 179, 180
Pravda, Bratislava, 34
Pravda, Moscow, 99, 129, 140, 150, 155, 174
Pražák, Professor Albert, 66, 67
Prchala, General Lev, 58
Prchlík, General Václav, 44, 45, 130, 131
Prešov, 89

"Radio Free Europe", 141

Rákosi, Mátyás, 94
Reportér, 7, 52
Richta, Radovan, 7
Rudé právo, 19, 42, 88, 94, 97, 105,
  115, 150, 161
Rybarpole, 21

Šalgovič, Viliam, 168
Sartre, Jean-Paul, 4
Schörner, Field Marshal Ferdinand,
  66
Sedláková, Mária, 34
Šejna, General Jan, 43, 44–47, 130
Šik, Ota, 5, 13–15, 37, 43, 102
Široký, Viliam, 19
Škvorecký, Josef, 6
Slánský, Rudolf, 2, 25, 31, 49, 50,
  67
Slavík, Václav, 6
Smrkovský, Josef, 42, 48, 57, 65–68,
  76, 94, 98, 102, 118, 149, 151,
  162, 174, 176
Sofia, 48
Solzhenitzyn, Andrei, 26
Špaček, Josef, 86
Stalin, Josef, 2–3, 19, 24, 49, 50, 59,
  61, 97, 184
Štrougal, Lubomír, 180
Student, 55, 98, 141
Sulek, Miroslav, 158

Švestka, Oldřich, 88, 90, 94, 150,
  161
Švermová, Marie, 49
Sviták, Ivan, 3, 54–55
Svoboda, General Ludvík, 57–61,
  147–49, 158, 159, 170, 173–77,
  186

Tábor, 45
Tito (Josip Broz), 2, 50, 132, 153
Třebíč, 60
Trybuna Ludu, 129

Ukraine, 88
Ulbricht, Walter, 93, 94, 151–55
Uzhgorod, 142

Vaculík, Ludvík, 27, 28, 116
Vlasov, General Andrei, 66, 67
Vltava River, 76
Voltaire, 55

Warsaw, 92, 129, 132

Yakubovsky, Marshal Ivan, 100, 148
Yepishev, General Aleksei A., 97

Zápotocký, Antonín, 8
Zhdanov, Andrei A., 5